D0016046

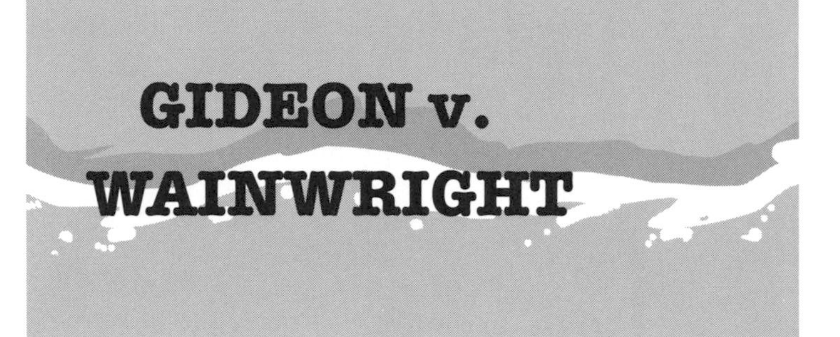
GIDEON v.
WAINWRIGHT

Gideon v. Wainwright

AND THE RIGHT TO COUNSEL

by
Paul B. Wice

Historic Supreme Court Cases
FRANKLIN WATTS
A Division of Grolier Publishing
New York London Hong Kong Sydney
Danbury, Connecticut

Library of Congress Cataloging-in-Publication Data

Wice, Paul B.

Gideon v. Wainwright and the right to counsel / Paul B. Wice

p. cm. — (Historic Supreme Court cases)

Includes bibliographical references and index.

Summary: Discusses the principle of the right to counsel for all defendants, the case of Gideon v. Wainwright, and the significance of the Supreme Court's decision regarding that principle.

ISBN 0-531-11231-4

1. Gideon, Clarence Earl—Trials, litigation, etc.—Juvenile literature. 2. Wainwright, Louie L.—Trials, litigation, etc.—Juvenile literature. 3. Right to counsel—United States—Juvenile literature. [1. Gideon, Clarence Earl—Trials, litigation, etc. 2. Wainwright, Louie L.—Trials, litigation, etc. 3. Right to counsel.] I. Title II. Series.

KF228.G53W53 1995

345.73'056—dc20 95-11290

[347.30556] CIP AC

Printed in the United States of America

6 5 4 3 2 1

CONTENTS

Chapter 1
A JAILHOUSE LAWYER

It is easy to forget that no matter how important a Supreme Court decision may turn out to be, it started out as a dispute between two adversaries. In the case of *Gideon v. Wainwright*, an impoverished ex-convict and part-time drifter named Clarence Earl Gideon challenged Louie L.Wainwright, director of the Florida Division of Corrections.

In 1961, Gideon was confined to a state prison in Raiford, Florida, serving a five-year sentence for attempted burglary. Gideon contested his conviction because the state of Florida had refused to provide him an attorney to represent him during his trial, and he had been forced to defend himself. While in prison, Gideon appealed his conviction through the Florida Supreme Court, but the appeal was unsuccessful. Then, he turned to the U.S. Supreme Court and asked them to hear his case.

THE MAN

Clarence Earl Gideon did not on the surface possess particularly heroic characteristics. At the time of his arrest for attempted burglary, he was living in Bay Harbor, Florida, a seedy suburban community on the outskirts of Panama City. Gideon was a somewhat sickly, middle-aged man who had been unable to hold down a regular job. He did not look well physically, though he had never been robust. At fifty-one years of age, he appeared much older. His weathered face and gaunt frame—he was six feet tall and barely 140 pounds—seemed to reflect a hard life.

Recently hospitalized in Louisiana, he had left a state medical facility there to return to Bay Harbor. Gideon knew from past experience that he might find several eager gambling partners at nearby Tyndall Air Force Base. According to his own statements, he planned to make some money gambling while recuperating in Bay Harbor from his illness.

Located in the panhandle of Florida, Bay Harbor was a depressing community just outside Panama City boundaries. It closely resembled the poor, "tobacco road" towns scattered throughout the rural South. Bay Harbor was distinguished primarily by the air pollution that the town's largest employer, The International Paper Company, produced. The rest of the town consisted of some rundown buildings, a store, a bar, and the Bay Harbor Poolroom.

Clarence Gideon's early life was neither pleasant nor uneventful. It was filled with poor health, bad luck, and sporadic run-ins with the law. Gideon was born August 30, 1910, in Hannibal, Missouri. He was raised primarily by his mother and, after

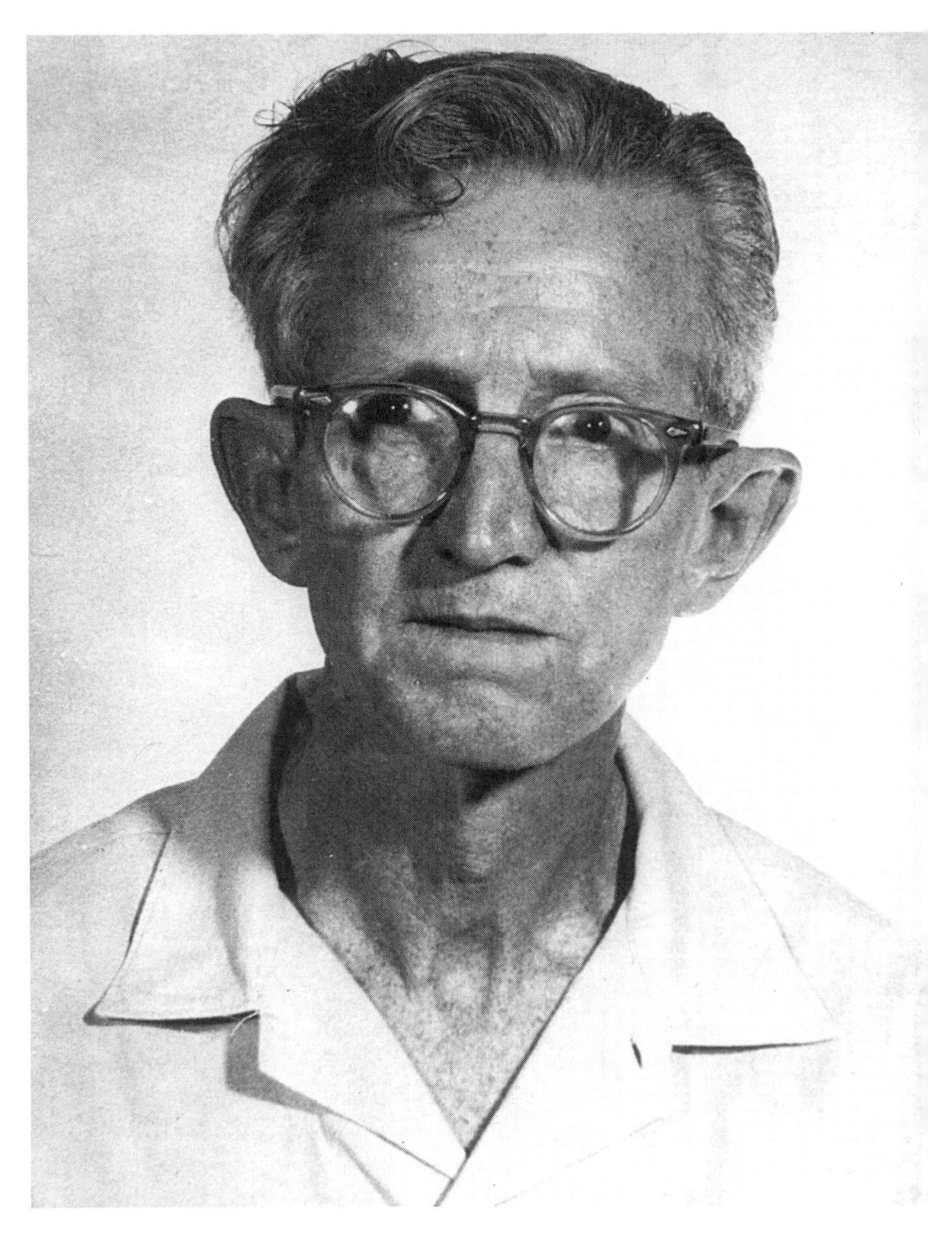

Clarence Earl Gideon

his father died when Gideon was three years old, a stepfather, in a fairly strict Baptist, working-class environment. Clarence Gideon never felt he fit into this setting, and he ran away from home at the age of fourteen.

Clarence Gideon had his first confrontation with the law soon thereafter. Found guilty of burglarizing a country store for some new clothes, he spent the next year in a Missouri reformatory. In the following thirty-five years, Gideon was convicted of the following four crimes: 1928, burglary in Missouri, sentenced to a ten-year term and paroled after three years; 1934, possession of government property (a federal conviction), sentenced to three years in prison; 1940, burglary in Missouri, sentenced again to a ten-year term. He escaped from prison in 1943, was captured the next year, served the full term, and was released in 1950; 1951, burglary in Texas, sentenced to two years in prison and released on September 25, 1952.

Following his release from prison in 1952, Gideon appeared to try to lead a more conventional life. For the next nine years, he avoided any entanglements with the police. During that time, however, he was plagued by serious health problems and an erratic employment record. In 1954, he underwent surgery for partial removal of a lung damaged earlier by tuberculosis.

On a more positive note, in 1955, Clarence Gideon got married. By 1961, his wife Ruth had six children, five from previous marriages. He tried to support his new family by working as a mechanic, but his lung problems returned and he spent most of 1959 in the hospital. Without his paycheck, his wife had to rely on a meager state welfare check of $81 a month. Following another serious operation, Gideon left Louisiana at the beginning of 1961 and began his brief, now historic, visit to Panama City.

On the surface, Gideon appeared to be a typical repeat-offender, a lawbreaker who started his lawbreaking early in life and continued to have trouble conforming to society's rules. On closer examination, however, Gideon, though handicapped by poor health and a forbidding criminal record, was attempting by the early 1950s to provide for his economically distraught family. He had indicated some aptitude for mechanical work and labored briefly, with skills he had learned in prison, as an electrician and auto repairman.

Clarence Gideon's previous experiences with the criminal justice system had also allowed him by 1960 to assume the role of "jailhouse lawyer." A jailhouse lawyer is an inmate who teaches himself the law in order to work for his release from prison. Gideon had not only worked on his own legal problems but he had also assisted other inmates with their appeals. He explained that "There's no real lawyers in here now. I guess I know more than most, and I help out. I have one boy in here [Raiford State Prison] that can't read or write. I wrote a letter to the Supreme Court of Florida for him asking them to appoint an attorney to write him a petition for habeas corpus. They accepted that letter as a petition and denied it without a hearing, so I wrote the whole thing over and sent it to the Supreme Court of the U.S."[1]

Gideon's unfortunate encounters with public agencies, ranging from state and federal justice organizations to numerous welfare and medical facilities over the years, had ingrained in him a reflexive dislike of government. He believed strongly that public officials, especially those in the state of Florida, were prejudiced against the underclass.

THE INCIDENT

It was shortly before dawn on June 3, 1961, when a Panama City police officer making his rounds noticed the front door of the Bay Harbor Poolroom slightly ajar. After investigating the scene more closely, he discovered that a window at the rear of the building had been shattered, and a cigarette machine and jukebox had apparently been robbed.

A bystander informed the policeman that he had looked through the storefront window a short time earlier and had seen a man in the poolroom—an acquaintance named Clarence Gideon. On the basis of this information, Gideon was arrested and subsequently indicted for breaking and entering with intent to commit a misdemeanor, which is a felony under Florida law.[2] (A misdemeanor is a less serious crime in which the defendant usually cannot receive a sentence of over a year; a felony is a more serious crime where the accused faces imprisonment of over a year.)

THE TRIAL

Clarence Gideon's trial commenced an August 4, 1961, in the Circuit Court of the Fourteenth Judicial Circuit of Florida (Bay County) before Judge Robert L. McCrary, Jr. Because Gideon's most recent courtroom and prison experiences had been especially scarring, he was insistent that the only way to escape the clutches of the state's oppressive prison system was to have a lawyer represent him.

Brought before Judge McCrary, Gideon rose and asked the court to appoint counsel to represent him. Gideon argued that because he was destitute, he could not afford to pay a lawyer. He went on to say that he believed that the U.S. Supreme Court had stated that people in his position were entitled to be represented by an attorney.

The judge listened patiently to the defendant's request and promptly denied his application. Under Florida law and federal constitutional precedents, the court was required to appoint counsel to represent a defendant only when the person was charged with a capital offense, a crime for which the defendant faced the possibility of the death penalty. For any lesser offense, including those that could result in lengthy periods of jail time, the state was unwilling to provide an attorney.

A trial proceeded quickly. Without a state-appointed lawyer, Gideon was forced to defend himself in front of the jury. He had to convince them that he was innocent, or at least show that the evidence presented by the state prosecutor, William Harris, failed to prove his guilt beyond a reasonable doubt. Gideon did his best during the trial; he cross-examined the prosecution's witnesses and introduced several of his own to confirm his side of the story.

How well did Clarence Gideon represent himself in the courtroom? Without the means to post bail, Gideon was in jail during the entire pretrial period. He was, therefore, unable to conduct any background investigation in preparation for trial. When the trial began, it was evident that the judge was trying to help Gideon defend himself as much as possible. Nevertheless, he failed to inform Gideon of his right to question each juror for possible bias, readily accepting Gideon's overall conclusion that "They [the jurors] suit me all right, your Honor."[3] When Gideon attempted to cross-examine the prosecution's principal witness, Henry Cook, the man who said he had seen Gideon inside the poolroom shortly before the break-in was discovered, Gideon engaged in an aimless argument, a reflection of his lack of legal expertise. Gideon brought forward eight witnesses for his defense, but they added little to his case. Gideon even made a closing argument to the jury.

The jury, however, failed to believe Gideon and found him guilty. Twenty-one days after the trial had begun, Clarence Gideon was sentenced. Taking Gideon's prior criminal record of several burglary convictions into consideration, the judge gave him the maximum penalty of five years' imprisonment.

After sentencing, Clarence Gideon began serving his five-year term at Raiford State Penitentiary. Still without legal counsel, Gideon soon started preparing to appeal his case to the Florida Supreme Court. Relying on his prior experience as a jailhouse lawyer and his familiarity with the prison's law library, Gideon completed a petition for habeas corpus and mailed it to the state's highest court, in Tallahassee. (Habeas corpus, "to produce the body," refers to the necessity or requirement of having to charge a person with a specific crime before the state can arrest and/or imprison him.) Gideon's argument was simple: the trial court's refusal to appoint a lawyer to represent him violated his constitutional rights.

Without offering an opinion or explanation, the Florida Supreme Court denied his petition. It was time for Clarence Gideon to turn to the federal courts.

TURNING TO THE FEDERAL COURTS

Although the state of Florida's legal system had resolutely denied his appeal and rejected his "right to counsel" argument, Clarence Gideon was enough

Raiford State Penitentiary, the Florida prison where Clarence Gideon served time

of a jailhouse lawyer to know the federal courts might hear his case. The federal courts will allow appeals from a state court system (1) when an appellant can raise a federal issue, and (2) after an appellant has exhausted all of the remedies available in the state system. If a prisoner like Clarence Gideon were to appeal to the federal courts, he would have to show that a major part of the appeal would focus on an issue linked to the Constitution.

Gideon had little trouble designating his case's constitutional issue—the right to counsel, which he believed was rooted in the Sixth Amendment's guarantee of assistance of counsel. Although this Bill of Rights provision applied only to federal prosecutions, the Fourteenth Amendment, added to the Bill of Rights in 1868, declared that states were also prohibited from depriving any person of life, liberty, or property without due process of law. There was a growing body of cases that argued that the Sixth Amendment's right to counsel requirements should be included in the Fourteenth Amendment's due process clause, a clause that affected state criminal proceedings. That is, if a defendant did not qualify to have a court-appointed lawyer under the Sixth Amendment because his case was a state, not a federal, case, then that defendant should qualify under the due process clause.

If a case involved a capital offense or fell within the so-called special circumstances rule, then the state would be obligated to provide assistance of counsel. What about less serious cases in which the defendant was capable of attempting to conduct his own defense? Gideon believed that the U.S. Supreme Court should extend the Sixth Amendment's right to counsel provision to all state defendants. Would the Supreme Court agree with this jailhouse lawyer named Clarence Gideon?

Although Gideon was confident that he had raised the required constitutional questions to satisfy the Supreme Court's jurisdictional restrictions, he was not sure that the Court would be willing to accept his appeal and grant certiorari. Certiorari is a writ, or order, from a superior court (e.g., U.S. Supreme Court) to a lower court (e.g., U.S. Court of

Appeals) calling up the record of proceedings. It signifies that the appeal has been granted and the case will be heard. Unlike the federal circuit court of appeals and nearly all state appellate courts, which are required to hear cases brought to them, the U.S. Supreme Court has the discretionary power to select only those cases it wishes to hear. The only cases that the Supreme Court is required to hear are the minimal number of appeals falling in their original jurisdiction. The Constitution defines such cases as either those "affecting ambassadors or other public ministers and consuls and those cases in which a state shall be a part."

Congress gave the Supreme Court the power to select its cases as part of the Judiciary Act of 1925, which substituted petitions for certiorari in place of mandatory appeals. The justices came up with the informal rule that four votes are required for a case to be selected. In a conference, at least four of the nine justices must agree that a case deserves to be granted full consideration by the entire Court; a date for oral argument is then scheduled.

The main reason for granting the Supreme Court this discretionary power was the steadily increasing number of appeals. The Court is capable of hearing and deciding only 150 to 200 cases a year. As the number of appeals exceeded their capacity, they had to devise some way to screen the cases.

By the early 1960s, when Gideon entered the federal system following his hearing before the Florida Supreme Court, the U.S. Supreme Court was receiving about two thousand cases a year. The Court could accommodate only one out of every ten appellants. (By the 1990s, the yearly number of appeals climbed to over five thousand, reducing the odds to fewer than one out of every twenty-five appellants' being heard.)[4]

IN FORMA PAUPERIS AND HOW IT WORKS

In addition to the depressing odds that practically assured that the Supreme Court would not decide to hear his case, Gideon also faced the problem of how to maneuver successfully through the complicated federal appeals process without a lawyer to help him. Despite its unwillingness to require states to provide counsel in criminal proceedings, the Supreme Court had been sensitive to the problems of those impoverished who wished to have their cases heard on appeal.

In the early 1930s, Chief Justice Charles Evans Hughes instituted a process called "in forma pauperis," most commonly referred to as "ifp's," for indigent, or impoverished, appellants. The chief justice also permitted people using an ifp's petition to file a single, handwritten copy. Paid petitions, in contrast, were almost always typewritten, filed in multiple copies (usually forty), and completed with the learned assistance of counsel.

Chief Justice Earl Warren, who took his seat on the bench in 1953, continued the Court's commitment to carefully considering the ifp's. Warren warned his law clerks who processed these appeals that "it is necessary for you to be their counsel, in a sense."[5] The Supreme Court also added that it will "make due allowance for technical errors so long as there is substantial compliance."[6]

Clarence Gideon's own petition in pauperis was written in pencil on notebook paper. Michael Rodak, Jr., assistant clerk of the Supreme Court at the time, was responsible for processing the in forma pauperis petitions and checking that they

In an effort to help impoverished appellants, Chief Justice Charles Evans Hughes simplified the federal appeals process.

satisfied the Court's Rule 53, which deals with the filing of ifp's. Although Gideon's petition was written in an overly legalistic style and filled with basic errors, Rodak determined that Gideon had satisfactorily complied with the applicable rules, particularly the crucial requirement that the appeal be filed within ninety days of the lower court decision.

Gideon's petition to the Supreme Court was one of approximately 1,500 received during the 1961–62 term. The Court would grant certiorari and hear only about 3 percent of these petitions, dismissing the overwhelming majority as frivolous.

The initial screening of the petitions is the responsibility of the chief justice's three law clerks. After each petition has been reviewed, one of the clerks drafts a brief memo on each case, summarizing the essence of the appellant's claim and any additional critical information. This memo is then circulated to all nine members of the Court. In the unusual case where the clerk believes that a case raises an especially interesting question, he notifies the chief justice, even before the other justices have seen the memo. If the chief justice agrees with the law clerk's assessment, the state authorities challenged in the appellant's brief will be asked to file a response to help clarify the legal issues and factual information.

Clarence Gideon had the good fortune to have his ifp's motion attract the attention of a Court clerk, who quickly notified Chief Justice Warren, who agreed that the Florida prisoner was raising a most interesting issue. The chief justice instructed the clerk's office to write to the Florida attorney general and direct the state to respond to Clarence Gideon's petition by April 7, 1962. The writer of this particular petition was unaware of this major step taken to address his complaints.

Chief Justice Earl Warren served as chief justice of the Supreme Court from 1953 to 1969.

THE STATE OF FLORIDA'S RESPONSE

Florida attorney general Richard Ervin turned the letter from the Supreme Court clerk Rodak over to one his assistants, Bruce R. Jacob, and directed him to respond by the deadline. On April 9 the Court received a thirteen-page brief from Jacob that reiterated the state's earlier position that under the earlier *Betts v. Brady* ruling, decided just twenty years earlier, Gideon was not entitled to trial counsel because he failed to show that the required "special circumstances" existed. The assistant attorney general explained that "Petitioner Gideon has made no affirmative showing of any exceptional circumstance which would entitle him to counsel under the Fourteenth Amendment. . . . There has been presented no evidence of petitioner's maturity or capacity of comprehension. Petitioner merely alleges that he was without funds, that he pleaded not guilty and that he requested court-appointed counsel, while being tried on a non-capital charge. The petition contains no allegations as to petitioner's age, experience, mental capacity, familiarity or unfamiliarity with court procedure, or as to the complexity of the legal issues presented by the charge. Petitioner has made no showing of unfairness or of a lack of fundamental justice in the trial proceedings. In fact, his petition is notable for its lack of material allegations such as would entitle him to counsel under the Fourteenth Amendment. Since there have been no allegations as to exceptional circumstances, the presumption must be indulged that the trial proceedings were fair and just."[7]

As required by the Supreme Court, Gideon received a copy of the state's brief and was notified that he could write a reply. On April 21, the Supreme Court received Gideon's four-page reply, again in pencil, repeating his original argument that he was entitled to a lawyer at his trial, and that without one, he had not received fair treatment.

It was time for the Supreme Court to decide if it wished to hear Gideon's appeal and grant certiorari. During formal conferences held every Friday, the Court discusses cases heard in oral argument earlier that week, as well as what cases it will hear in future weeks. Gideon's case would be discussed during the Friday conference scheduled for June 1, 1962. With twenty-six petitions for certiorari on the appellate docket, ten pauper's (or ifp's) applications on the miscellaneous docket, and an additional three petitions for rehearing, it was a very busy time for the Court. The discussions proceed in extreme secrecy, with the chief justice presiding over a full, yet orderly, agenda.

The results of the deliberations were announced the following Monday, on June 4. Among the decisions was the granting of Clarence Gideon's petition for a writ of certiorari. Included was the specific request that opposing counsel in the case discuss, both in their briefs and oral argument, the following question: "Should this Court's holding in *Betts v. Brady* be reconsidered?"

Why was Clarence Gideon's case one of the successful 3 percent of the ifp's to be granted certiorari? Like so many important events in history, it is often a matter of being in the right place at the right time. For Gideon, it was just that—mostly a matter of good timing.

Ever since the *Betts v. Brady* decision, some members of the Court, concerned members of the bar, and legal scholars had been vocal in their displeasure with this decision. In the two decades following this controversial case, professional comments, especially in law reviews, had been critical and growing in fervor. Several members of the Court, including Earl Warren, William O. Douglas, and Hugo L. Black, who wrote the dissenting opinion in *Betts*, had begun to urge its overruling. One legal scholar asserts that the chief justice had even gone so far as to instruct his law clerks to look for a case that would permit the Court to decide if the *Betts* decision should be overturned.[8] At both the state and federal level, there had been much criticism of the *Betts* ruling. Several decisions chipped away at the ability of *Betts* to deny free legal counsel to indigent defendants in state criminal trials, and specifically attacked the "special circumstances" requirement.

Despite the strong sentiment for reconsideration of *Betts*, it was not clear that the Court wanted to overturn completely the 1942 decision. Some justices believed that overruling it only twenty years after *Betts* was handed down might make the Court appear unstable or impulsive. Additionally, several justices had reasonable fears about the practical impact of the case on the criminal justice system. Anyone familiar with the criminal courts knew that the overwhelming majority of defendants—estimated at between 70 to 80 percent of all defendants—were indigents, and would be in need of publicly assisted legal defense. Overturning *Betts* would put a significant financial and organizational burden on state and local justice systems.

Regardless of whether the justices were in favor of overturning the *Betts* decision or simply tinkering with the "special circumstances" rule, the Supreme Court realized that it was time to address the issue of indigent state defendants and their right to counsel. It was for this reason that, during their Friday conference on June 1, the justices voted overwhelmingly to grant certiorari to Clarence Gideon's petition.

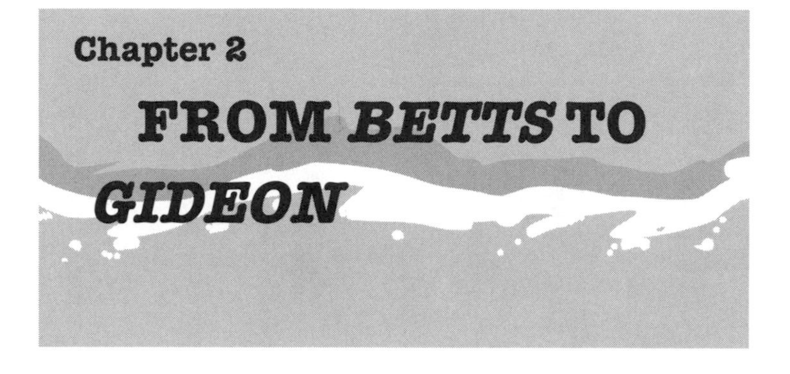

Chapter 2

FROM *BETTS* TO *GIDEON*

When Chief Justice Earl Warren and the rest of the Supreme Court agreed to hear Clarence Gideon's appeal, the justices and attorneys from both sides had to begin thinking of how they would handle the 1942 Supreme Court decision of *Betts v. Brady*.[1] This decision, written by Justice Felix Frankfurter, who was still a member of the Court in 1962, served as a formidable precedent. *Betts v. Brady* had to be overruled or somehow distinguished if Gideon was to succeed in establishing a right to counsel in state felony trials.

Because the American legal system is a common-law system, decisions such as *Betts* are made to establish a legal standard. Courts in the United States (especially the appellate divisions, which must rule on issues of law) depend on the judicial doctrine of stare decisis, or "following precedents." The term is derived from the Latin, and means "to stand by what has been decided." Although earlier rulings or precedents are not ironclad or inflexible,

Justice Felix Frankfurter penned the historic Betts v. Brady *majority opinion in 1942.*

courts and judges understand that people expect a consistency in the law and a building on past decisions. The Court, however, can and does upon occasion change its collective mind and overrule itself.

Before the *Gideon* case in 1963, what was the Court's understanding of the right to counsel? Professor Mason Beaney and other constitutional scholars point out that the issue of the right of poor people to free legal representation is a relatively recent development in American constitutional law. Professor Beaney writes that "the Sixth Amendment guarantee that an accused person may have the assistance of counsel for his defense was originally construed as providing only the right to retain a lawyer, a right that had sometimes been unavailable under English law at the time the Bill of Rights was adopted (1789). Nevertheless, the constitutional right to the assistance of counsel was not held to be binding on state governments, which conduct the vast majority of American criminal prosecutions. Only a few states guaranteed in their constitutions the right to appointed counsel; more commonly, state and federal statutes provided for appointed counsel under particular circumstances, while judicial discretion to appoint counsel was sometimes exercised in special cases. In most jurisdictions counsel was appointed in none but the most serious cases, often only when the crime was punishable by death."[2]

POWELL v. ALABAMA

The Supreme Court first confronted the right-to-counsel problems of indigent defendants in *Powell v. Alabama*[3] in 1932. The Scottsboro case, as it was also called, brought a group of impoverished farm boys national prominence. The specific incident that sparked the controversy occurred on a slow-moving freight train, winding its way through Tennessee with a slight pass through a corner of Alabama—specifically Scottsboro, Alabama—on March 25, 1931. On the train were two groups of teenagers—one black, one white. There was a dispute, a fight ensued, and when the train arrived in Scottsboro, nine young black men on the train were charged with raping two white women.

If found guilty, the defendants, whose ages ranged from thirteen to twenty-one, faced the death penalty. None of these illiterate, out-of-state, penniless youngsters could afford an attorney. When the trial judge called on the local bar to volunteer their legal services, he was forced to wait anxiously for a response. He waited for six days without a single attorney coming forward. Then, he appointed "all the members of the bar" to represent the defendants. Six days later, the judge's proclamation had still produced no visible legal assistance. On the day the trial was to begin, the judge finally appointed a lawyer to handle the young men's combined defense. That lawyer, Stephen Roddy, was a Chattanooga attorney of limited experience with an occasional drinking problem.[4]

In the trials that followed, each of which was completed in a single day, eight of the accused were found guilty and sentenced to death. After their conviction, the defendants appealed their case through the Alabama judicial system and finally reached the U.S. Supreme Court in 1932. They argued that they had been denied effective counsel because of the lateness of the appointment of their attorney and because of that attorney's questionable competence and noticeable reluctance to represent them.

Writing the majority opinion for the Supreme Court, Justice George Sutherland agreed with the defendants, concluded that they had been unconstitutionally denied counsel, and reversed their convictions. Justice Sutherland believed that because the defendants were young and uneducated, because they had been put on trial in a hostile community, and because they feared for their very lives, they required assistance of effective counsel. He went on to say that their rights under the due process clause of the Fourteenth Amendment had been violated.

In the majority opinion of the Court, the ruling established and clarified the importance of providing counsel to a defendant. They explained, "Left without the aid of counsel he may be put on trial without a proper charge, and convicted upon incompetent evidence, or evidence irrelevant to the issue or otherwise inadmissible. He lacks both the skill and knowledge adequately to prepare his defense, even though he may have a perfect one. He requires the guiding hand of counsel at every step in the proceedings against him. Without it, though he be not guilty, he faces the danger of conviction because he does not know how to establish his innocence. If that be true of men of intelligence, how much more true is it of the ignorant and illiterate, or of those of feeble intellect."[5]

FROM *POWELL* TO *BETTS*

What exactly was the constitutional significance of the *Powell v. Alabama* decision in terms of right to counsel guarantees for indigent defendants? It soon became clear that the *Powell* decision was not intended to require counsel for defendants in *all* state criminal cases. Instead, it was a narrow decision, confined to the case's specific circumstances and the unusual characteristics of the Scottsboro boys. The Court had simply stated that in this particular set of facts, there was a denial of effective counsel, which violated both the due process guarantees imposed upon the states by the Fourteenth Amendment and the general requirements of the Fifth Amendment, which required due process.

The *Powell* decision and its importance as a meaningful precedent was limited by Justice Sutherland's concluding remark. He said, "All that is necessary now to decide, as we do decide, is that in a capital case, where the defendant is unable to employ counsel, and is incapable of adequately making his own defense because of ignorance, feebleness, illiteracy or the like, it is the duty of the Court, whether requested or not, to assign counsel for him as a necessary requisite of due process of law."[6]

Despite the limited nature of the ruling, *Powell v. Alabama* was a historic decision. For the first time in Supreme Court history, justices had been willing to intervene in a state criminal trial and reverse a defendant's conviction due to unfair procedures that had violated due process of law. Nevertheless, the *Powell* case was only the first step in guaranteeing due process protection to all defendants in state trials.

The next opportunity to measure the impact of the *Powell* decision and to clarify the Court's thinking on the right to counsel issue occurred in the case of *Johnson v. Zerbst* in 1938. In contrast to *Powell*, which was a state criminal proceeding, *Johnson v. Zerbst* was a federal case. John Johnson, a U.S. marine, was charged with passing counterfeit money. He was tried and convicted without the assistance of counsel. Because of the federal nature of the case, only the Sixth Amendment was applicable in Johnson's appeal. The Supreme Court, with Justice Hugo L. Black writing the majority opinion, found Johnson's argument persuasive and agreed to reverse his conviction.

Throughout his career on the bench, Justice Hugo L. Black strongly supported the rights of defendants.

Justice Black, speaking for a bare majority of five justices, concluded his decision by stating that the Sixth Amendment does not allow the federal courts in any of their criminal proceedings to deprive a defendant of his life or liberty unless he has (or chooses to waive) his right to the assistance of counsel.[7]

Although the *Johnson v. Zerbst* opinion may have issued a strong declaration of support for the right of federal defendants to assistance of counsel, it provided little help for defendants like Clarence Gideon, in any of the fifty state criminal court systems. State defendants, who comprise the overwhelming majority of criminal cases in the country, anxiously awaited a court decision more relevant to their circumstances.

It continued to be the case that if a person was accused of a capital offense or was sufficiently mentally defective, the 1932 *Powell* case could prove to be applicable, and a lawyer would have to be appointed. Otherwise, for nearly every defendant accused of a crime in a state court, the Sixth Amendment's right to counsel provision did not apply; thousands of individuals, like Clarence Gideon in Florida, would have to conduct their own defense.

BETTS v. BRADY

In 1942, in *Betts v. Brady*, ten years after *Powell v. Alabama*, the Supreme Court reexamined the issue of withholding counsel from indigent state defendants charged with noncapital crimes. With this case, the Court had the opportunity to review and possibly to expand on its earlier, limited *Powell* decision.

Smith Betts, a farmer in rural Maryland, was

the defendant in the case. Charged with robbery, he was unable to afford his own lawyer. The state of Maryland, which offered assistance of counsel only to indigents in capital offenses, rejected his request for an attorney. The presiding judge in the case informed Betts he would have to act as his own attorney. During his trial, Betts cross-examined prosecution witnesses and brought in several individuals to support his version of the incident and verify his alibi. Nevertheless, at the end of the trial, Betts was found guilty and sentenced to eight years in prison.

In reviewing the transcript of the trial, the Maryland Court of Appeals concluded that the proceeding had been fairly routine. The appeals court judge believed that Betts had been able to defend himself adequately.

The Supreme Court, in reviewing Betts's appeal, agreed with the lower court that he had satisfactorily argued his case. Voting six to three against Betts, the Court declared that the Constitution, specifically the Fourteenth Amendment, did *not* require the states to appoint an attorney in every criminal case when a defendant requested one. The Court acknowledged that while it was perfectly acceptable for a state, of its own will, to provide legal defense for its indigent defendants, the U.S. Constitution did not require such action. (Several states had, in fact, recently created public defender and assigned counsel programs.) Not only did the *Betts* decision return the appellant to the Maryland correctional system for several more years, it also announced to the country that the Sixth Amendment applied only to federal trials.

Before making their ruling, the Court examined

the two major precedents for this case—*Powell v. Alabama* and *Johnson v. Zerbst*. Betts had argued that *Johnson* raised the question of "whether the constraint laid by the Sixth Amendment upon the national courts expresses a rule so fundamental and essential to a fair trial and so to due process of law that it is made obligatory upon the states by the Fourteenth."[8] The Court rejected this argument. The second precedent, *Powell v. Alabama*, was also found inapplicable and rejected. In *Powell*, the group of young men on trial were young and illiterate, and were therefore found to be incapable of defending themselves. In this case, there were "special circumstances" that prevented the defendants from adequately defending themselves. In the *Betts* case, however, the defendant was a forty-three-year-old adult of average intelligence, whose courtroom performance was proficient enough for the Court to conclude that his trial had not denied him the "fundamental fairness" guaranteed by the Fourteenth Amendment.

The *Betts* decision produced a sharply divided Court. William O. Douglas and Frank Murphy joined with Justice Hugo L. Black in his strongly worded minority opinion. Fortunately for Clarence Gideon, Justice Black stayed in good health and remained on the Court for another thirty years. In *Betts*, however, Black had to be content with writing an energetic dissent. He would have to wait for history to catch up with his belief that the Fourteenth Amendment should incorporate the right to counsel guaranteed in the Sixth Amendment and that it should extend this protection to state criminal proceedings.

The basis for Black's dissent was his firm belief that the right to counsel in a criminal proceeding was a "fundamental" due process right that was required under the Fourteenth Amendment. In concluding his dissent, Black argued that not providing counsel is a practice that "subjects innocent men to increased dangers of conviction merely because of their poverty. Whether a man is innocent cannot be determined from a trial in which, as here, denial of counsel has made it impossible to conclude, with any satisfactory degree of certainty, that the defendant's case was adequately presented."[9]

What, then, was the major significance of the *Betts* decision, and what kind of precedent did it set for the defense attorneys who tried to help Clarence Gideon obtain a new trial? Three major conclusions could be drawn from the *Betts* decision: (1) although the right to counsel in criminal proceedings was an important procedural element, it was not sufficiently critical to be called "fundamental," and therefore did not require the Sixth Amendment to be nationalized through the Fourteenth Amendment's due process clause;* (2) a state need provide counsel only in criminal cases where it was clearly indicated that "special circumstances" showed the defendant was unable to competently defend himself; and (3) the Supreme Court would continue to monitor and supervise state criminal proceedings to ensure that no instances would be permitted that would "shock the universal sense of justice" (*Rochin v. California*, 1952) or be offensive to the common and fundamental ideas of fairness and right.

**Nationalized* means that the Supreme Court believes that a specific element of the Bill of Rights—the original ten amendments to the Constitution—is so critical to the American system of justice that it is to be applied to the states as well as the federal government through the "due process clause" of the Fourteenth Amendment.

FROM *BETTS* TO *GIDEON*

Thus, in 1942 and in the following two decades before the *Gideon* case, the U.S. Supreme Court continued to be interested in a defendant's right to counsel in criminal proceedings, but only when one or more of the previously stated conditions existed. This position forced the Court to monitor and evaluate the right to counsel issue case by case. If the particular facts of a case satisfied the "special circumstances" test, or the trial court's actions were clearly offensive to the principles of fundamental fairness, then, and only then, would the Court act. Both standards were vague and provided little concrete guidance as to the inclinations of the Court on the question of right to counsel for noncapital state criminal cases.

Initially the Court believed that, with the *Betts* decision, they had rejected a rigid rule in favor of a more flexible one that tied to the specifics of a case. In the twenty-one-year span between *Betts* and *Gideon*, however, the Court seemed less, not more, likely to rule against a right to counsel argument. The Court seemed to develop its own set of right to counsel guidelines that found special circumstances lacking in case after case.

Why did the Court find that "special circumstances" were lacking in so many right to counsel cases after *Betts*? It is possible to see how the Court could reason that defendant after defendant was not significantly harmed by the absence of an attorney. Yale Kamisar, a law professor at the University of Michigan, writes: "The failure of the unrepresented defendant to develop a satisfactory theory or, if he does, to support it with adequate evidence—likely consequences of being without the aid of counsel inside and outside the courtroom—makes the case seem exceedingly simple and the defendant look overwhelmingly guilty."[10] The logic becomes circular: if a defendant appears guilty—which is likely if he did not benefit from legal representation during the trial—then the best lawyer in the bar could not have helped the defendant.

Fortunately for indigent defendants, the Supreme Court, beginning in the mid-1950s with the arrival of the new chief justice Earl Warren, began consistently to find that "special circumstances" *did* exist, and furthermore required the states to retry the case, this time providing the defendant with assistance of counsel. By 1961, the Court even went so far, in the case of *Hamilton v. Alabama*, to remove the capital case requirement as a formality. The Supreme Court also appeared to be more sensitive to the obstacles that faced indigent defendants in state criminal proceedings, especially in their efforts to appeal a conviction.

The Supreme Court showed new attitudes toward impoverished defendants under the leadership of Chief Justice Earl Warren. The case that best illustrated this was *Griffin v. Illinois*.[11] Instead of relying on the due process requirements of the Fourteenth Amendment, in *Griffin* and subsequent decisions, the Supreme Court used that amendment's equal protection clause to require states to provide indigents with certain resources for their defense and for their appeal. The *Griffin* case struck down an Illinois statute that granted free trial transcripts to indigents only for review of constitutional questions and when the defendant had received a death sentence. The Court held that the right of indigents to meaningful appellate review was denied unless they were furnished trial transcripts in any appeals.

Decisions such as *Griffin* set the stage for a reexamination of the critical issue of whether states were constitutionally obligated to provide assistance of counsel in criminal cases. By the early 1960s, it was clear that the Court was becoming frustrated by the *Betts* "special circumstances" test. Law professor Francis Allen wrote that right to counsel cases decided under the *Betts* formula at this time were "distinguished neither by the consistency of their results nor the cogency of their argument. . . . The rule therefore seems vulnerable to fundamental criticism and so long as it persists, the law of the subject will remain in the state of unstable equilibrium."[12] Allen's scholarly attack on the Court was echoed in several other articles, all decrying the unworkable nature of the *Betts* special circumstances rule. The Court itself continued to decide in favor of every state defendant who raised a denial of counsel issue.

The most vocal supporter of the *Betts* decision, Justice Charles Evans Whittaker, found himself increasingly on the losing side. In a 1960 dissenting opinion in *Hudson v. North Carolina*, Whittaker somewhat bitterly noted that the majority opinion overruled a state conviction of a defendant who had no counsel "without so much as mentioning *Betts v. Brady*."[13] In April 1962, about the time the *Gideon* case reached the Supreme Court, two crucial changes in personnel shifted the Court even further away from the *Betts* decision.

On April 1, Justice Whittaker retired from the Court. Four days later, Justice Felix Frankfurter, who had voted with the majority in *Betts* and believed strongly in supporting the states' control over their criminal court proceedings, suffered a stroke and did not participate in the *Gideon* case.

Led by an activist chief justice and aided by three associate justices from the minority *Betts* opinion, the Court seemed poised to reconsider the *Betts* decision. At about the same time, Clarence

The Court that decided to hear Clarence Gideon's case: (clockwise from upper left) Byron R. White, William J. Brennan, Jr., John M. Harlan, Potter Stewart, William O. Douglas, Hugo L. Black, Chief Justice Earl Warren, Felix Frankfurter, and Tom C. Clark

Earl Gideon, with a request handwritten from his Florida penitentiary cell, began a legal journey that would ultimately result in victory not only for himself but for every impoverished defendant in the country who had been denied the right to counsel.

Chapter 3

LEGAL REPRESENTATION AT LAST

Following the joyous news that the Supreme Court would hear his appeal, Clarence Gideon was faced—finally and happily—with the task of selecting an attorney to argue his case. The chief deputy clerk of the Court notified Gideon that he should communicate to the Court his desire to be provided with legal representation. On June 18, 1962, Gideon's formal request reached the Supreme Court.

The choice of who would be appointed to represent Gideon was left completely up to the members of the Court. With no strict guidelines governing the selection process, the Court usually selects prominent lawyers who are known professionally to at least one, and often several, of the justices. In the past, former law clerks to the justices, law professors, and practitioners have been selected. The justices of the Court also consider where an attorney is from, because they like to choose someone from the defendant's part of the country.

The selection of Clarence Gideon's attorney was made during the Court's Friday conference on June 22, just before they were to break for their summer recess. After the conference, Chief Justice Warren told the clerk of the Court, John F. Davis, that the justices had chosen a lawyer named Abe Fortas to represent Clarence Gideon. The appointment would be made public the following Monday. At that time, it was up to Davis to inform the attorney of his appointment and determine if there was any reason he would be unable to accept the assignment. Although attorneys rarely turn down such an offer, it was important to avoid embarrassing the Court with a public rejection from a surprised counsel. After some difficulty locating the appointee, Davis tracked him down in Dallas and gave him the news. Fortas accepted the assignment with pleasure and asked a few questions about the major legal issues in the case.

From all accounts, Abe Fortas appeared to be an excellent choice. His professional history was impressive. He had been a law professor and later worked at the prestigious Washington law firm of Arnold, Porter and Fortas. Fortas had the respect of both Chief Justice Warren and Justice Douglas. Douglas knew him from his work on the case of *U.S. v. Durham* and Warren was familiar with his work on the Advisory Committee on Criminal Rules. During these committee meetings, Fortas had earned a reputation for being a strong advocate of the rights of the accused. Despite his lofty position at one of the most powerful law firms in Washington, D.C., he was on record as believing that it was a lawyer's professional obligation to represent any indigent client assigned to him.

Abe Fortas, the lawyer appointed by the Supreme Court to represent Clarence Gideon

THE *DURHAM* CASE: A NEW DEFINITION OF INSANITY

It was Abe Fortas's efforts on the *Durham* case that probably most convinced the Court that he was the ideal candidate to defend Clarence Gideon. In 1951, the D.C. Circuit Court of Appeals appointed Fortas as counsel for a man named Monte Durham, who had broken into the home of Alger Hiss's brother, in Georgetown, D.C. (Alger Hiss was a former high official in the U.S. Department of State who was accused of being a Communist agent in 1948.)

Durham's medical record showed that he had been a patient in a D.C. mental hospital three times, and twice had been pronounced insane; it seemed sensible that he plead "not guilty" by reason of insanity. Although Durham had been consistently evaluated by psychiatrists as "medically" insane, his condition did not fit the legal definition of insanity formulated in England in 1843 and used by nearly all U.S. courts. In the eyes of the law back then, a person was deemed insane if he did not understand the consequences of his acts and could be said not to know right from wrong.

In Durham's defense, Fortas argued before the court that the definition of legal insanity had to correspond more closely with contemporary knowledge of psychiatry and aberrant behavior. Fortas explained that, even if a person could distinguish right from wrong, his behavior might be affected by a mental condition that could override his ability to differentiate between the two. Fortas's argument was accepted, and Monte Durham was found innocent by reason of insanity. Basing its opinion on Fortas's carefully researched and very persuasive brief, the circuit court created a new, more flexible doctrine stating that "an accused is not criminally responsible if his unlawful act was the product of a mental disease or defect."[1]

Although the *Durham* decision directly affected only the District of Columbia and federal district courts, it was a major legal victory. After the Depression in the 1930s and before *Durham*, Abe Fortas was a highly respected lawyer in Washington circles. Following *Durham*, he became nationally recognized by justices and legal scholars across the country.

ABE FORTAS'S BACKGROUND

What kind of man was behind this admirable professional reputation? This question has proved to be difficult to answer.

Fortas, despite his brilliant intellect and remarkable professional accomplishments, was always a rather puzzling individual. Nicholas Katzenbach, U.S. attorney general under President Lyndon Baines Johnson, said in 1983, "I have never met anyone who was brighter than Abe Fortas. I used to think if I ever got into serious, serious trouble, I would want Abe to represent me."[2] In her prize-winning *Abe Fortas*, author Laura Kalman wrote that "all those who knew Fortas professionally would have agreed he was among the most talented lawyers of his generation—neither they nor any of his friends, however, ever claimed to understand him."[3]

Fortas's roller-coaster life began in Memphis, Tennessee. An exceptional student and violinist, Fortas attended Southwestern University, a small, local liberal arts college. He went on to Yale Law School, where he won praise for his legal brilliance and gained the respect of one professor in particular—William O. Douglas. Douglas encouraged Fortas to join him in Washington, the center of the

New Deal, a program of innovative laws and organizations that President Franklin D. Roosevelt designed to combat the great Depression during the 1930s. Tempted instead by academic life, Fortas worked for three years as a law professor at Yale and as a key policy maker at both the Agriculture Adjustment Administration (AAA) and then, with Douglas, at the Securities and Exchange Commission.

In time, Fortas left academics to devote himself full-time to his work in Washington. He was soon appointed chief deputy at the Interior Department. In 1946, he left the government to establish a law firm. Fortas teamed up with two other New Dealers, Thurmond Arnold and Paul Porter, to found a high-powered law firm in the nation's capital. Combining legal acumen with inside connections, the firm promised its clients excellent results in disputes involving the federal government.

In 1948, Lyndon Baines Johnson asked Fortas for help in a bitter Texas primary battle for the U.S. Senate. Johnson's opponent was trying to challenge the election results through court action, charging blatant voter fraud. Fortas got the courts to affirm Johnson's controversial victory, and he remained a close friend and personal lawyer to LBJ throughout his career.

Later, in 1963, when John F. Kennedy was assassinated and Johnson took office, Fortas was a leading member of his transition team. Two years later, after being rebuffed several times, President Johnson finally succeeded in getting Fortas to accept a nomination to the Supreme Court. Abe Fortas was sworn in on October 4, 1965.

When Chief Justice Earl Warren announced his resignation from the Supreme Court in 1968, LBJ nominated his trusted friend for the most powerful

President Lyndon B. Johnson introduces his appointee to the Supreme Court, Abe Fortas, at a 1965 press conference.

(Right) Part of the four-page letter that Abe Fortas sent Chief Justice Earl Warren to announce his resignation from the Supreme Court in 1969

CHAMBERS OF
JUSTICE ABE FORTAS

Supreme Court of the United States
Washington, D. C. 20543

May 14, 1969

The Honorable Earl Warren
Chief Justice
Supreme Court of the United States
Washington, D. C. 20543

My dear Chief Justice:

I am filing with you this memorandum with respect to my association with the Wolfson Family Foundation, and a statement of the reasons which in my judgment indicate that I should resign in order that the Court may not continue to be subjected to extraneous stress which may adversely affect the performance of its important functions.

As you know, I [illegible] report or announc[illegible] municated [illegible] Court, but rather to resign in the hope [illegible] the Court to proceed with its vital work free from extraneous stress.

There has been no wrongdoing on my part. There has been no default in the performance of my judicial duties in accordance with the high standards of the office I hold. So far as I am concerned, the welfare and maximum effectiveness of the Court to perform its critical role in our system of government are factors that are paramount to all others. It is this consideration that prompts my resignation which, I hope, by terminating the public controversy, will permit the Court to proceed with its work without the harassment of debate concerning one of its members.

I have written a letter asking President Nixon to accept my resignation, effective as of this date.

I leave the Court with the greatest respect and affection for you and my colleagues, and my thanks to all of you and to the staff of the Court for your unfailing helpfulness and friendship. I hope that as I return to private life, I shall find opportunities to continue to serve the Nation and the cause of justice which this Court so ably represents.

Sincerely,

Abe Fortas

position on the Court. However, Abe Fortas's close relationship with President Johnson, by this time an increasingly unpopular figure who had decided not to run for reelection, prevented Fortas's confirmation. The nomination was withdrawn and Fortas remained on the Court as an associate justice.

Fortas's problems continued into the next year when it was discovered that he had engaged in several questionable practices involving an old friend, Warren Wolfson, who had recently been convicted of criminal charges involving illegal stock manipulations. Although the Justice Department never made any direct charges against Fortas, he resigned from the Supreme Court under a cloud of suspicion, his professional career permanently discredited. Upon reflection, it might be fair to say that serving as Clarence Gideon's lawyer marked the zenith of Abe Fortas's legal career.

FORTAS AND THE *GIDEON* CASE

As soon as Fortas accepted his appointment as Gideon's attorney, he began to mobilize his law firm's considerable resources to help him. He turned to Abraham Krash, one of the firm's most talented younger attorneys, to direct the research effort. Krash had previously performed a similar function in Fortas's defense of Monte Durham and the reconstituted definition of legal insanity. Both Fortas and Krash had extremely busy schedules; with the oral argument set for only seven months away, in mid-January, 1963, the two Abes feverishly set to work to complete their written briefs.

If Fortas's ultimate goal in mounting the appeal was not only getting Gideon's conviction reversed but also overturning the *Betts v. Brady* decision, then he had to be sure of Gideon's competence during his trial. If Gideon's defense efforts in the initial trial could be deemed incompetent, then he would fall within the guidelines of the "special circumstances" exception established in *Betts v. Brady*. And if the transcript indicated that Gideon himself had indeed been incompetent, Fortas knew that he would have "to advise the Court and to argue that his conviction should be overturned on the special circumstances doctrine without the necessity of reconsidering the basic holding of *Betts*. . . . It would have been my duty to do this even though it would have been frustrating to the Supreme Court as well as annoying and even though it would have meant that I was handling a more or less routine criminal case."[4]

After closely reading Gideon's trial transcript, Fortas was relieved to find that Gideon could in no way be placed within the narrow confines of the special circumstances doctrine. Gideon had made a decent, yet flawed, effort in a difficult case, and he had received the gentle assistance of the trial judge. In fact, during the preparation of their appellate brief, Fortas and Krash interviewed Judge McCrary, the judge who had presided over Gideon's trial. He said that Gideon had done "as well as most lawyers would have done in handling this case."

Fortas also requested that Clarence Gideon send him an autobiographical statement to confirm his minimal competence, which would clearly put him outside the *Betts* guidelines. Gideon responded with a twenty-two page letter summarizing his feelings about the American legal system. Gideon wrote: "I have no illusions about law and courts or the people who are involved in them. I have read the complete history of law ever since the Romans first started writing them down and before the laws of religions. I believe that each era finds a [*sic*] improvement in law each year brings something new for the benefit of mankind. Maybe this will be one of those small steps forward, in the past thirty-five years I have seen great advancement in Courts in penal servitude. Thank you for reading all of this. Please try to believe that all I want now from life is the chance for the love of my children the only real love I have ever had."[5] The letter convinced Fortas of Gideon's competence.

The next challenge for Gideon's lawyers was formulating the argument that the *Betts* case should be overruled, on the grounds that the Fourteenth Amendment's due process clause necessitated counsel's being appointed for a defendant accused of a serious offense. They would argue that legal representation was essential to a fair trial.

Fortas understood the practical implications for states if *Betts* was overturned. If the Court decided to reverse *Betts*, local justice systems would be forced to provide attorneys for all indigent defendants, a group that tended to monopolize the criminal courts already. In response to this argument against overturning *Betts*, Fortas reasoned that overruling *Betts* and the special circumstances rule would not interfere with states' rights, but improve the states' standing in the federal system. His brief contended that the *Betts* decision "had caused conflict between the federal and state courts because of the case by case review it entails and because it does not prescribe a clear cut standard which the court can follow."[6] Fortas concluded his argument by writing, "How corrosive it is for federal state relations to have a federal court tell . . . a state court judge later that he did not do an adequate job."[7]

For the *Gideon* case to truly change the way

state legal systems were run, Fortas and his team needed not just to win but to win as close to a unanimous ruling as possible. The task would be a difficult one; the Supreme Court is traditionally very reluctant to reverse itself on a constitutional question, especially one as important as a defendant's right to counsel. The Court was also reluctant to appear easily changeable by reversing itself on a case that had been decided only twenty years earlier.

Fortas and Krash worked diligently on the brief throughout the summer, and a draft was completed by Labor Day. Not completely satisfied, Fortas spent another week cramming in the firm's library, and then another two days in a New York hotel room composing a detailed outline that he turned over to Krash for the final draft.

Gideon's lawyers' fifty-three-page brief of five sections was filed with the Court on November 21, 1962. The brief was signed by Fortas, Krash, and Ralph Temple, an associate at the firm. In a footnote, they acknowledged the "valuable assistance of John Hart Ely, a third year Yale law student." Copies were mailed to opposing counsel in the Florida attorney general's office as well as Clarence Gideon in his prison cell in Raiford. Fortas and his associates impressed the justices with having done a masterful job.

THE OPPOSING COUNSEL: ARGUING FOR THE STATE

Opposing Abe Fortas and his superb team of young attorneys was the state of Florida, defending the state's position. Their goal was to convince the Supreme Court that Clarence Gideon had received a constitutional trial and should remain in Raiford

State Penitentiary to serve out the rest of his sentence.

The Florida attorney general's office had selected one of its youngest and least experienced attorneys to handle the case. Their choice, Bruce R. Jacob, was only twenty-six years old and had never been before the Supreme Court. Jacob's academic and professional accomplishments, next to Abe Fortas's, were modest. He graduated from Florida State University and then received a law degree from Stetson Law School in St. Petersburg, Florida. After trying private practice for a few months, Jacob joined the state attorney general's office. He had been working in the criminal division there for only two years when the *Gideon* case reached his desk.

After Gideon's petition for review reached the attorney general's office, Reeves Bowen, head of the criminal appeals division, assigned Jacob to the *Gideon* case. While Abe Fortas and his associates worked on the *Gideon* brief as a team, Bruce Jacob worked alone. The final draft of his brief was seventy-four pages long. In his brief, Jacob tried to convince the Supreme Court to refuse to use the *Gideon* case to overrule *Betts*. He argued that according to existing law, Gideon had not satisfied the special circumstances rule and had done a decent job in conducting his own defense; he therefore had not been entitled to an attorney. Jacob spent the remaining portion of his brief explaining why the federal system requires each state to construct its own rules for deciding which criminals are entitled to a guaranteed legal defense. Jacob concluded with the following warning: "If this Court should decide to overrule *Betts*, respondent respectfully requests that it be accomplished in such a way as to prevent the new rule from operating retrospectively."[8] On December 17, Jacob learned that oral argument had been set for January 14, 1963.

AMICUS CURIAE BRIEFS

After talking with a few of the more experienced lawyers in the criminal appeals division, Bruce Jacob decided to write the other forty-nine states to ask them to write amicus curiae (friend of the court) briefs in support of the Florida position. He imagined that most states would be troubled by the possibility of the U.S. Supreme Court's imposing the requirement that states provide counsel for indigents in all serious criminal cases. State and local politicians, concerned about the practical consequences of having to find funding for the additional legal expenses, would likely support an amicus brief that argued for the continued use of the *Betts* guidelines. In his letter, Jacob wrote, "If the minority can obtain one more vote, *Betts* will be overruled and the States will, in effect, be mandatorily required to appoint counsel in all felony cases. Such a decision would infringe on the right of the states to determine their own rules of criminal procedure."[9] Jacob's letter was approved and signed by Florida attorney general Richard W. Ervin and sent out to the attorney generals of the other forty-nine states.

The exact purpose of amicus briefs has always been somewhat confusing. Many people believe that these briefs, filed by organizations and individuals not part of the case, might provide the Court with useful expertise and experience. In recent years, however, amicus briefs have been simply an indicator of public opinion in cases involving controversial legal questions. Because the Supreme Court can be flooded with amicus briefs for highly publicized, emotional cases, a recent Court order permits these briefs to be filed only with the consent of all parties of the case. The exception, particularly relevant to *Gideon*, is the federal and state governments, which always have permission to file such briefs.

Jacob's optimism that his letter would rally support from other concerned states was misplaced. Only two states—Alabama and North Carolina—spoke up in favor of the Florida position. The letter did appear to influence the states, but not in the way Jacob had intended. Not only did Florida receive little support for its position, but twenty-two states filed amicus briefs supporting the other side!

This groundswell of support was not entirely spontaneous. Two attorney generals—Walter F. Mondale of Minnesota and Edward J. McCormack, Jr., of Massachusetts—had organized a carefully orchestrated and doggedly persistent campaign to urge their fellow attorney generals to sign on in support of Gideon. Mondale, generally credited with leading the entire movement, argued in his brief that the new constitutional right to counsel would be in effect only for future cases and would be limited to felony cases. Mondale and McCormack believed that modifying their demands would increase their chances of convincing all the states to sign the Massachusetts–Minnesota amicus brief.[10]

It is difficult to measure what impact the amicus briefs had in this case. The fact that only two states supported Florida's position, and twenty-two chose to endorse the overruling of *Betts* and a national right to counsel in criminal cases, had to have weakened Florida's argument that states' rights would be harmed if *Betts* was overturned. It was now up to the two sides to state their cases before the Supreme Court.

Chapter 4

REACHING THE SUPREME COURT

A confident Abe Fortas and an anxious Bruce Jacob entered Washington's imposing Supreme Court building on Monday morning, January 14, 1963. (Their case was not actually argued until the afternoon of the next day. The reading of several opinions in the morning and President Kennedy's State of the Union address in the afternoon delayed the proceedings.) The two attorneys were to face the nine members of the nation's highest court: Chief Justice Earl Warren and Associate Justices Arthur J. Goldberg, Byron R. White, Potter Stewart, William J. Brennan, Jr., Tom C. Clark, Hugo L. Black, William O. Douglas, and John M. Harlan.

The Court had received written briefs months earlier. On this day Fortas and Jacob would be adversaries during an oral argument lasting approximately two hours. Each attorney would be given an hour to present his argument and respond to the questions of the justices. They would also be permitted a brief opportunity of about five minutes to rebut the opponent's arguments.

Following this formal presentation, two additional speakers selected as "friends of the court" would be heard. First Lee Rankin representing the American Civil Liberties Union would speak in support of Clarence Gideon's appeal. As a highly respected former solicitor general, he knew most members of the Court. The amicus curiae advocate chosen to represent the state of Florida's position was the assistant attorney general for the state of Alabama, George D. Mentz.

Abe Fortas's performance during the oral argument was skillful. He and his associates had an inkling that most of the justices were leaning toward overturning *Betts v. Brady* and endorsing Gideon's appeal. The mere fact that the Court had granted certiorari offered strong evidence of their inclination. Additionally, several members of the Court, including Chief Justice Warren and Associate Justices Douglas and Black, had made their displeasure with the *Betts* special circumstances rule fairly clear.

During his oral argument, Fortas concentrated on what he described as the "narrow question" raised by Gideon's case—the constitutional necessity for overruling *Betts* and granting the Sixth Amendment's right to counsel to all defendants in state felony trials. He attacked the issue of states' rights by pointing out that thirty-seven states already provided counsel for the poor in all felony trials, eight others offered such assistance if requested, while five made no regular provision for counsel except in capital cases. He concluded by saying, "We may be comforted in this constitutional moment by the fact that what we are doing is a

Lee Rankin of the American Civil Liberties Union (ACLU) spoke to the Court as a "friend of the court" in support of Gideon's appeal.

deliberate change after twenty years of experience—a change that has the overwhelming support of the bench, the bar, and even the states."[1] Upon completing his eloquent argument, Abe Fortas stepped down and relinquished the podium to his youthful adversary.

Bruce Jacob was, naturally, very nervous about his first appearance before the U.S. Supreme Court. He must have felt like the underdog, like David against the giant Goliath. It didn't help to know that the Court would be critical of his position. Describing the memorable event, full of frustration and apprehension, Jacob said later, "I wanted to be honest. When they asked me whether there were some prisoners in Raiford [State Penitentiary] who should have had counsel, I had to say yes, because I had read some records and I knew there were. But the more honest I was, the more they kept putting me on the spot. . . . You could tell that they knew what they were doing, that they were awfully smart men, that they had the benefit of the best thinking of the country."[2]

THE CONFERENCE

On the Friday following an oral argument, all cases presented during the week are decided in a proceeding called "the conference." During this closed-door meeting with only the nine sitting justices in attendance, each case heard that week is discussed, debated, and ultimately decided. There is no official record kept of the discussion. No more than a few days after the conference, the chief justice decides who will write each case's majority opinion, if he is on the winning side. If the chief justice is not on the winning side, the justice from the winning side with the most years of service on the Court decides who will write the majority opinion. Over a period of several months, different justices will write the majority, concurring, and dissenting opinions.

Because of the way these conferences are conducted, no one can be sure what was said during Court discussions of the *Gideon* case. In the time between when the conference is held and the written opinion is formally announced, there can be a great deal of interaction among the justices. When opinions are circulated at the draft stage (and they frequently are), they can generate more discussion about a case. Before a justice officially signs on to a majority opinion or joins with a colleague in a concurring or dissenting opinion, he or she carefully reviews the draft opinion. After analyzing the draft, the justices may lobby one another to amend or alter an opinion. Because of the Court's cherished policies, no record of any debate during the conference itself or in the subsequent months when opinions in the *Gideon* case were being drafted was made public.

DELIVERING THE OPINION

The Supreme Court does not give any notice before announcing its decisions. The Court maintained its traditional silence about when a decision in *Gideon* would be made public and, of course, what that decision would be. Exactly two months after discussing the *Gideon* case in their conference, the Court was ready to hand down its decision. Abe Fortas and Bruce Jacob, expecting to have to wait at least another month, were surprised that a decision had been reached. On March 18, 1963, the Court was ready to make legal history.

The willingness of a Court to directly overrule an earlier decision has been historically a fairly rare occurrence, with only one hundred such direct reversals in the Court's first 150 years of operation. A reversal is news, and a crowd gathered at the Supreme Court building that blustery March morning, anxiously awaiting word from the Court, as they often did on decision Mondays.

Consistent with nearly two centuries of tradition, the Supreme Court delivers all of its opinions orally. Because all cases to be presented are announced in ascending order of the seniority of the justice delivering the opinion, Hugo L. Black, a justice for over twenty-five years, spoke last that day.

The first four cases established a pattern for a potential reversal of the *Betts* decision. In the case immediately preceding *Gideon*, Justice Douglas delivered the opinion of the court in the *Douglas v. California* case. A six-to-three vote had decided that indigent prisoners were entitled to free counsel for their appeals. If the right to an attorney could exist for defendants at the appellate stage in state courts, then how could it not also be provided at the trial stage?

It was at this time that Justice Black stated, "I have for announcement the opinion of the Court in number 155, Gideon against Wainwright." (The case no longer involved one H. G. Cochran, who had resigned as director of the Florida Division of Corrections. His replacement was Louie L. Wainwright, who, despite his brief relation to the actual case, would forever have his name associated with the historic opinion.) Justice Black stated that Clarence Gideon's case "raised a fundamental question, the rightness of a case we decided twenty-one years ago, Betts against Brady, and we reach an opposite conclusion." Justice Black and his associates on the Court had voted for the right of a defendant in a state criminal proceeding to be

In 1962, during the process of Gideon's appeal, H. G. Cochran, right, resigned as director of Florida's prison system and Louie L. Wainwright, left, was named to replace him.

guaranteed counsel. Clarence Gideon and Abe Fortas had won their case.

In addition to Black's majority opinion, there were three additional opinions written by justices Douglas, Clark, and Harlan. All three, however, were concurring opinions. Each emphasized the writer's specific reasons for joining the majority in overturning *Betts*, and for affirming Gideon's right to counsel. Chief Justice Warren must have been pleased; the Court had rendered a unanimous decision that convincingly overturned the landmark *Betts v. Brady* decision. The nine-to-zero decision would significantly ease problems from defiant state officials hoping to escape from the obligation of providing legal counsel for impoverished defendants.

ANALYZING THE OPINION

The decision to overturn *Betts* came as little surprise to the legal community. Announced just before *Gideon*, the *Douglas v. California* decision was a radical departure from existing procedures that required states to provide counsel not just during the trial but for all appeals.[3] The Court's trend toward guaranteed counsel was clear; the only question was how Justice Black and his colleagues would dispose of the *Betts* precedent.

When Hugo L. Black wrote his majority opinion for *Gideon v. Wainwright*, he understood that he had to dispose of the *Betts* precedent with some care. In his opinion, Justice Black devoted most of his energy to explaining why the *Betts v. Brady* precedent had to be reconsidered and ultimately overruled.

Justice Black began with the facts in the *Betts* case, which he found to be strikingly similar to the *Gideon* case. Like Gideon, Betts had requested and was denied assistance of counsel in a state court. Like Gideon, Betts had argued that the denial of free counsel violated his Fourteenth Amendment due process rights and had taken his case to the Supreme Court. Betts's appeal, however, had been rejected. The Court had believed that the right to counsel was not fundamental to a defendant's due process.

In the second half of his opinion, Justice Black attempted to show that the *Betts* decision was a departure from such earlier Supreme Court decisions as *Powell v. Alabama* in 1932 and *Johnson v. Zerbst* in 1938. According to Black, these cases showed clearly that appointment of counsel for all defendants, including indigents, was a fundamental right essential to a fair trial and must be applied to the state courts. When the Court ruled on the *Betts* case, they had simply erred in ruling that the Sixth Amendment's guarantee of a right to counsel was not fundamental and essential to a fair trial.

Justice Black then returned to the more narrow issue of whether the right to counsel guarantees of the Sixth Amendment should apply to state as well as to federal criminal trials. Even before *Betts* was decided, he stated, there were strong precedents that indicated the Court's desire to require that counsel be appointed to all defendants. Although the *Powell v. Alabama* ruling had some limitations, "its conclusions about the fundamental nature of the right to counsel are unmistakable." Black then quoted from the 1938 case of *Johnson v. Zerbst* in which the Court wrote that "The assistance of counsel is one of the safeguards of the Sixth Amendment deemed necessary to insure fundamental human rights of life and liberty. . . . The Sixth Amendment stands as a constant admonition that if the constitutional safeguard it provides be lost, justice will not still be done."[4]

Justice Black further argued that "reason and reflection" should compel the Court to reverse the *Betts* decision. How can a legal system operate fairly and constitutionally if the state's case is argued by a prosecutor trained in the law while the defendant's case is argued by a layman, financially incapable of hiring a lawyer? How will the defendant know how to prepare his case, bring forth and examine witnesses, compose opening and closing statements to the jury, or influence the judge's charge to the jury? Justice Black answered, "From the very beginning, our state and national constitutions and laws have laid great emphasis on procedural and substantive safeguards designed to assure fair trials before impartial tribunals in which every defendant stands equal before the law. This noble ideal cannot be realized if the poor man charged with crime has to face his accusers without a lawyer to assist him."[5]

Finally, Justice Black added that amicus briefs were the proof: two states supported Florida's position and twenty-two states supported Gideon's position. The time had come for a reversal of *Betts*. The ruling was "an anachronism when handed down and should now be overruled."

DIFFERING VIEWS: THE CONCURRING OPINIONS

When Justice Hugo L. Black wrote the majority decision to reverse the Florida Supreme Court's ruling and permit Clarence Gideon a retrial, with court-appointed counsel, he spoke for a unanimous Court. Several other justices, however, wished to set down for the record their own specific reasons for reversing the *Betts* decision.

Although the Gideon *ruling was unanimous, Justice John M. Harlan wrote a concurring opinion for the record.*

The justice least satisfied with Justice Black's majority opinion was Justice John M. Harlan. While he agreed that *Betts* needed to be reversed and that the right to counsel was a fundamental provision of the Bill of Rights, he felt the need to write a separate opinion to give the *Betts* case a "more respectful burial." Harlan acknowledged that his response might have differed somewhat from the majority opinion because, unlike Black, he had not been a member of the Supreme Court when *Betts* was decided in 1942.

For Harlan, the *Betts* decision was not an abrupt break with the cases that came before it. Instead, it was part of an evolution. Harlan observed that the Supreme Court decisions after *Betts* over time had "substantially and steadily eroded" *Betts*'s "special circumstances" rule (which provided counsel only to indigent defendants with mental, emotional, or intellectual inadequacies) and rendered it unrealistic. Justice Harlan concluded that "to continue a rule which is honored by this court only with lip service is not a healthy thing and in the long run will do disservice to the federal system."[6] In his concurring opinion, Harlan recognized that he and the other members of the Court "have come to recognize that the mere existence of a serious criminal charge constituted in itself special circumstances requiring the services of counsel."[7]

The last purpose of Justice Harlan's concurring opinion was to emphasize his belief in the federal system of justice and the necessity for carefully deciding, on a case-by-case basis, which specific Bill of Rights provisions should be applied to the states through the Fourteenth Amendment. Justice Harlan was very hesitant about coercing the states into automatically adopting all of the Bill of Rights guarantees. Harlan feared that that approach "would disregard the frequently wide disparity between the legitimate interests of the states and of the federal government, the divergent problems they face, and the significantly different consequences of their actions."[8]

The second justice to write a concurring opinion, Justice William O. Douglas, held a view quite different from Justice Harlan's. While Harlan was uneasy about forcing state governments to provide free counsel, Douglas would have liked Black's majority opinion to have gone even farther, making the entire Bill of Rights enforceable against the states. Douglas also urged the members of the Court, and Harlan in particular, to realize that when the guarantees set forth in the Bill of Rights are applied to the states under the Fourteenth Amendment, they are of equal strength and character as when they are applied to the federal government, not merely "watered-down versions."

The third and final concurring opinion was written by Justice Tom C. Clark. He believed that the distinction the Court made between providing counsel in capital cases and not providing it in noncapital cases was no longer justified. To Clark, the distinction made little sense as a matter of either logic or constitutional law. And, since states had to provide counsel in capital cases, he saw no reason why they should not also have to provide counsel in noncapital cases. He concluded his opinion saying "that the Constitution makes no distinction between capital and noncapital cases. The Fourteenth Amendment requires due process of law for the deprival of 'liberty' just as for deprival of 'life,' and there cannot constitutionally be a difference in the quality of the process based merely upon a supposed difference in the sanction involved."[9]

Justice Tom C. Clark felt that the Gideon ruling did not go far enough in securing defendants' rights.

THE POLITICS OF OVERRULING

After reading Justice Black's convincing arguments, one wonders why it took the Court so long to reach such an obvious decision. Why had the Court waited twenty years to correct what Justice Black had argued since his vigorous dissent in the original *Betts* decision in 1942? And why did the Court reverse *Betts* with Clarence Gideon's case, of all cases?

To answer these questions, it might be helpful to look at the approaches used by the Court to overrule a precedent. There are three general methods. Law professor Philip Kurland offers the following three of the Court's approaches: (1) "changing conditions"; (2) "tests of experience"; and (3) "the requirements of later cases." In the first approach, the Court underscores the fact that circumstances have changed over time. With this method, the Court can reject a precedent and concede the original decision's rightness at the same time. In the second approach, the Court rejects a precedent after it fails to pass "the test of experience." In the third approach, used in most of the Court's overrulings, the Court criticizes the earlier decision for errors or inconsistencies in its reasoning. It was this last approach that the Court used in the *Gideon* case.[10]

In the late 1940s and throughout the 1950s, many cases reaching the Supreme Court raised the same right to counsel issue that was ultimately resolved in the 1963 *Gideon* decision. So why did the Supreme Court decide on the right to counsel issue when it did? Political realists are quick to answer that it is simply a question of membership changes on the Court. It is true that, with Justice Frankfurter's retirement in 1962, no sitting judges from the *Betts* majority remained on the bench.

Frankfurter was known as a strong supporter of the special circumstances rule, and he had been a vocal opponent of any movement to nationalize the Bill of Rights through the Fourteenth Amendment.

In an interesting article that addressed the issue of timeliness in the *Gideon* decision, Abe Krash discounted the change in membership argument. He pointed out that the *Gideon* decision was unanimous. In fact, several of the justices who had often shared Justice Frankfurter's views of stare decisis and the limited role of the Supreme Court with regard to the rights of the accused voted with the majority.

Krash argued that there were several other factors that explain much more accurately the timing and the outcome of the *Gideon* decision. First, he wrote that the Court "had become convinced by its own experience that the existing rule governing the assignment of counsel in state criminal prosecutions—the special circumstances test of *Betts v. Brady*—was simply not a workable standard. The Court had made a valiant effort to give content to the rule. But each decision led to new qualifications. . . . In short, the special circumstances test was too ambiguous, too subjective, too difficult to administer."[11]

Krash's second point was that the Supreme Court was no longer troubled by the federalism issue of coercing states into appointing counsel for all defendants. It seemed that most states did not need coercing. At the time of the *Gideon* decision, the large majority of states already provided, in one form or another, for the appointment of counsel in all felony cases. Only five states, in the South, did not make provision for appointment of counsel in all felony cases.

The third and most fundamental reason offered

by Krash to explain the timing of the *Gideon* decision was that it lay at the heart of the "Due Process Revolution" of the Warren Court. According to Krash, this Court, named for Chief Justice Earl Warren, "had become convinced that a fair system of justice requires that every man have the assistance of a trained spokesman, whether the trial occurs in a federal or a state courthouse. . . . The *Gideon* decision cannot be regarded as an isolated phenomenon. It is part and parcel of the whole corpus of constitutional law relating to state criminal procedure created by the Supreme Court during the past quarter of a century."[12]

As is true for most historic Supreme Court decisions, the opinion can be read narrowly or broadly. Read narrowly, the *Gideon* decision provided Clarence Gideon the opportunity for a retrial in Florida. Read broadly, the *Gideon* decision unraveled many more complex right to counsel issues.

Chapter 5
THE IMMEDIATE IMPACT

Gideon v. Wainwright was not the only Supreme Court decision announced on Tuesday, March 18, 1963. That day, the Court handed down decisions for three other cases that touched on right to counsel issues and clarified the Court's commitment to providing competent legal assistance to all felony defendants during the trial stage and the appellate process. Although the three cases, *Draper v. Washington*,[1] *Lane v. Brown*,[2] and *Douglas v. California*,[3] relied primarily on the equal protection clause of the Fourteenth Amendment and focused on the appellate process, they are nevertheless historically associated with *Gideon* and deserve explanation.

In the first case, *Draper v. Washington*, indigent defendants who had been represented by appointed counsel at trial were convicted of a felony and sentenced. Acting as their own counsel (pro se), the defendants filed notices for appeal and requested a free transcript of their trial record. In a hearing on these requests, the trial judge, following state law, rejected their request because he found the appeals lacked merit. The Supreme Court found the state of Washington's procedures had violated the equal protection clause of the Fourteenth Amendment. The Court stated that the trial judge's power to deny such an appeal was excessive, and that every defendant was entitled to at least "a record sufficiently narrative of what had transpired at the trial."[4]

The second case, *Lane v. Brown*, is a continuation of the development of the Fourteenth Amendment and equal protection principles, which were clearly laid out in the 1956 decision of *Griffin v. Illinois*.[5] The *Griffin* case held that the state's refusal to furnish an indigent defendant with free transcript, necessary for his appeal, deprived him of his Fourteenth Amendment rights. The *Lane* case differed from *Griffin* in only two minor ways: (1) the appellants were appealing not the conviction itself but the denial of petition for a writ of coram nabis (coram nabis, literally "before us ourselves," refers to a writ directing another branch of the same court to correct an error); and (2) the state did not deny free transcripts outright but required that a public defender request them. In this particular case, the public defender had denied Brown's request on the grounds that the state believed his appeal was without merit. Finding the first distinction irrelevant and the second unpersuasive, the Supreme Court unanimously rejected the state of Indiana's procedures.

The other decision announced on March 18 was *Douglas v. California*, a case that some legal scholars believed might prove to have as far-reaching an impact as the *Gideon* case. The defendants, who

Justice William O. Douglas, the author of the majority opinion of Douglas v. California

were represented by a public defender at their trial, were convicted of thirteen felonies. The defendants then dismissed their trial counsel, appealed, and requested a new counsel. The appellate court denied the request. Under a state law, such courts are permitted to deny appointed counsel if, after an independent investigation of the record, "in their judgment such appointment would be of no value to either the defendant or the court."[6]

Writing the majority opinion, Justice Douglas rejected the California law. He argued that the law discriminated against an indigent defendant, who was allowed the benefit of counsel only when the appellate court concluded that the appeal had merit, while a wealthy defendant could afford his own counsel to coerce the appellate court to hear arguments no matter how frivolous the appeal. Douglas summed up that there "is an affirmative duty upon the courts to appoint counsel for the appeal as of right, regardless of the merit of such an appeal or the seriousness of the offense."[7]

These three cases, combined with the *Gideon* decision, made March 18 a historic day for guaranteeing the rights of poor defendants. It was a particularly historic day for Clarence Gideon and other indigent defendants who sat in state prisons, after having been convicted at trials in which they had no counsel.

THE RETRIAL

The Supreme Court's ruling on the *Gideon* case on March 18 did not permit Clarence Gideon to walk out of Florida's Raiford State Penitentiary a free man. The opinion merely granted Gideon a retrial, with the assistance of counsel. It was altogether possible that, even with the help of a competent attorney, Clarence Gideon would still be found guilty of breaking into the Bay Harbor Poolroom.

Shortly after the Supreme Court decision was handed down, Abe Fortas wrote to Gideon about his upcoming trial and suggested that it might be in Gideon's best interest to be represented at that trial by a local Florida attorney. Fortas informed Gideon that he had already written to a Florida Civil Liberties Union attorney, Tobias Simon, about the possibility of becoming Gideon's new attorney. A highly respected Miami attorney, Simon was familiar with the case and had even signed the American Civil Liberties Union amicus curiae brief submitted to the Supreme Court for the *Gideon* case. Gideon seemed pleased, at least initially, by the possibility that Simon or one of his Civil Liberties Union colleagues would defend him.

In early May, Tobias Simon traveled to Raiford State Penitentiary to visit with Gideon and to begin planning a legal defense. Gideon was extremely agitated about his upcoming trial, and he told Simon he believed that the Supreme Court should have ordered his release from prison. He thought that the scheduling of a new trial violated the double jeopardy provisions of the Bill of Rights, and, furthermore, that the lengthy period of time since his arrest (by this time over two years) was in excess of the state of Florida's statute of limitations. In fact, Gideon was in error on both counts.

United States law holds that double jeopardy does not apply to a new trial awarded following a successful appeal. And the state of Florida's statute of limitations does not begin until after the appeals process has been completed. A final irritant, which further intensified Gideon's anger, was the fact that Judge Robert McCrary, Jr., the very same judge who had presided over his original trial, would also handle his second one. Gideon's efforts to shift venues to another jurisdiction for the retrial proved fruitless. The new trial was set for July

5, 1963, at the Circuit Court of Bay County in Panama City.

On the eve of the trial date, Tobias Simon and Irwin Block, another lawyer who had agreed to help on the retrial, traveled to Panama City to visit with the defendant and interview some witnesses. At this point, Gideon had become so upset over Florida's refusal to grant him an outright release that he refused to be represented by either Simon or Block.

When all three men appeared before Judge McCrary the next morning, Gideon again stated his refusal to accept the assistance of the two lawyers and informed the judge he was unprepared for trial. Convinced that he could not receive a fair hearing in Panama City, he repeated his wish to move the trial elsewhere and stated that he would plead his own case. This final demand visibly upset the judge. After a short time, tempers cooled and the judge was able to obtain Gideon's consent to being defended by Fred Turner, an experienced local criminal lawyer. The judge finally granted a one-month postponement for the new trial. A bail of one thousand dollars was set. Gideon, unable to raise the money, was returned to Raiford to await trial.

Sometime later, Tobias Simon reported back to the Florida Civil Liberties Union on the Gideon episode. Although he had found the entire experience frustrating, he was able to offer some insight into the individuals (one of whom was Clarence Gideon) whose names are associated with the nation's historic court decisions, but whose personal attributes hardly seem to qualify them for prominence. Simon wrote, "the great rights which are secured for all of us by the Bill of Rights are constantly tested and retested in the courts by the people who live in the bottom of society's barrel. . . . In the future the name "Gideon" will stand for the great principle that the poor are entitled to the same type of justice as are those who are able to afford counsel. It is probably a good thing that it is immaterial and unimportant that Gideon is something of a 'nut,' that his maniacal distrust and suspicion lead him to the very borders of insanity. Upon the shoulders of such persons are our great rights carried."[8]

Not only did Gideon's retrial feature the same judge as in the original trial but Gideon also faced the same prosecutor, William E. Harris. The team of prosecutors, which included Harris's boss, J. Frank Adams, and another colleague, J. Paul Griffith, appeared confident as the retrial began. A jury was selected after just an hour.

The primary witness for the prosecution, again, was Henry Cook, the man who had identified Gideon as being inside the pool hall that fateful morning. By attacking Cook's testimony, Gideon's attorney, Fred Turner, was able to cast doubt as to the accuracy of his early morning identification. He was also able to reveal that Cook was a convicted felon, something that he had lied about previously. Later in the trial, Turner accused Cook of being part of the group that had actually robbed the pool hall. Additional prosecution witnesses included the owner of the poolroom, Ira Strickland, Jr., arresting officer Duell Pitts, and cab driver Preston Bray. None of them could provide direct evidence of Gideon's guilt.

It was now the defense's opportunity to present their side of the case. Their first witness was J. D. Henderson, the owner of a local grocery store. Henderson stated that when Cook came into his store on the morning of June 3, he had told

Henderson that he wasn't sure whom he had seen in the poolroom, but he thought the person looked like Gideon. The defense's only other witness was Clarence Earl Gideon. To explain why he had so much loose change in his pocket, the defendant said that, when he was gambling, he always carried around a lot of coins to be ready for spontaneous opportunities. He closed his testimony with a final denial of any involvement in the robbery.

In the forty-five-minute closing argument, defense attorney Turner again raised the likelihood that Henry Cook was the actual guilty party, whose identification of Gideon was a ploy to hide his own involvement. It was nearly four thirty in the afternoon when the jury left the courtroom to decide Gideon's fate. An hour later, the jury returned to notify the judge that a verdict had been reached. They had found Clarence Earl Gideon not guilty. When Gideon learned of the jury's decision to free him after almost two years in prison, he was visibly moved. "Do you feel like you accomplished something?" a newspaper reporter asked. "Well I did,"[9] Gideon replied.

THE ISSUE OF RETROACTIVITY

Clarence Gideon was not the only defendant serving time in a state prison, having been convicted of a felony without the assistance of counsel. Abe Krash reported that, in Florida alone, "of the 8,000 prisoners in the State's penal institutions, 4,542 were convicted without a lawyer and by October 1963, more than 3,000 of these prisoners had filed petitions seeking review of their convictions on the authority of *Gideon*."[10] The Supreme Court, as well as other state and federal criminal justice agencies, was faced with the complex question of the *Gideon* ruling's retroactivity—how far back in time the

After winning his case, Clarence Earl Gideon returned to the Bay Harbor poolroom in Panama City, Florida, for a triumphant game.

decision should be applied. They had to consider if additional limitations should be applied to minimize the consequences of opening the constitutional floodgates to thousands of indigent defendants already in jail.

In fall 1963, the Supreme Court was forced to confront the ramifications of the *Gideon* decision for the first time. Ten Florida prisoners, convicted without assistance of counsel, petitioned for review of their state's refusal to grant them writs of habeas corpus. The Supreme Court, on October 14,

1963, sent the cases back to the Florida Supreme Court for reconsideration in light of the *Gideon* decision.

Florida bowed to public pressure and applied the Gideon rule to *all* of its inmates who had been convicted without counsel. By January 1, 1964, it was reported that nearly one thousand prisoners had been released outright from Florida's prisons because the prosecutors believed they could not be successfully retried. An additional five hundred were able to have retrials.[11] Lee Silverstein, a research attorney for the American Bar Association, reported that the state of Florida even enacted legislation to create a new office of public defender within each judicial circuit.[12]

Only a small minority of states argued that the *Gideon* decision should not be applied retroactively to all cases, but should be reserved for convictions without counsel only after March 1963. The general consensus on the retroactivity issue soon declared that the *Gideon* decision should apply only to defendants whose convictions occurred after Gideon's initial trial in 1961. Additionally, nearly all agreed that *Gideon* should also apply to all cases that raised the right to counsel issue awaiting disposition in any state or federal court when *Gideon* was decided by the Supreme Court, regardless of the date of the original conviction.

REACTION FROM POLITICAL AND LEGAL ORGANIZATIONS

Many Supreme Court decisions, such as the school prayer and abortion rights cases, are unpopular with large segments of the population. *Gideon v. Wainwright*, however, was received positively by the general public, the legal community, and state justice officials. The fact that the response to

Gideon was positive was fortunate, because carrying out the ruling had the potential of being extremely costly and complicated, as hundreds of thousands of defendants were affected. Among others, the *Washington Post* praised the decision, commenting "like the Gideon of old who was summoned by an angel of the Lord to lead Israel and overcome the Midianites, Clarence Earl Gideon of Panama City, Florida, championed the cause of justice for all indigent defendants. . . . It is intolerable in a nation which proclaims equal justice under law as one of its ideals that anyone should be handicapped in defending himself simply because he happens to be poor."[13]

To satisfy the dictates of the *Gideon* decision more completely, many states made immediate plans to redesign their right to counsel provisions. Lee Silverstein estimated that by 1964, at least twenty-six states had made significant changes in their appointment of counsel practices for indigent defendants. He also found many other states implementing reforms in particular counties. These changes tightened up the procedures by which counsel is offered and made it more difficult to waive one's right to counsel. Many states now require the judge to appoint counsel for a poor person before he even enters a plea to the indictment filed against him. In several states, such as Massachusetts, West Virginia, and North Carolina, the right to counsel can now be waived only with a signed document.[14]

The *Gideon* case made its greatest impact in the five southern states that had previously failed to appoint lawyers for indigent defendants in any case except one involving a capital offense or other special circumstances. Florida was the first of these five states to pass legislation creating a statewide

After the Gideon *ruling, the Ford Foundation funded programs to provide lawyers for indigents accused of crimes.*

public defender program. The remaining states—North Carolina, South Carolina, Alabama, and Mississippi—all modified their local procedures to assure that lawyers would be provided to the poor. In Alabama and Mississippi, for example, the legislatures responded to *Gideon* by assuring appointment and compensation of counsel for indigent defendants in all felonies at both the trial and appellate stages.

In addition to the actions of state governments around the country that made voluntary efforts to comply with the *Gideon* decision, several important legal organizations initiated programs for improving the quality of legal services for indigent defendants. The Ford Foundation offered grants of $2.5 million for a series of projects, most of which were operated by the National Legal Aid and Defender Association, designed to create model defender services programs in several cities. The American Bar Foundation and the Institute of Judicial Administration also began to focus on the problems of indigent defendants and their legal rights.

Judging by the positive reception throughout the nation to *Gideon*, it was obvious that the Supreme Court had been right in believing that the time had come to overrule *Betts* and grant all indigent defendants the right to free counsel in felony cases.

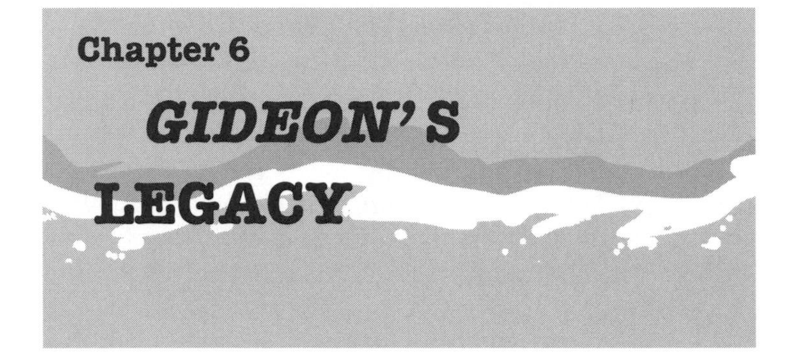

The importance of a Supreme Court decision is often measured by its impact on future cases. A decision that affects only cases closely related to the original case may be considered minor. A decision that affects a variety of other broader issues over time may be considered truly significant.

The process resembles the effect of tossing a stone into a peaceful lake. In Supreme Court cases of minor significance, it is as if a small pebble has been dropped directly into the water, making only a single wave of ripples that spreads a short distance out from the initial splash. In cases of major significance, it is more like a heavy stone has been forcefully thrown into the water, resulting in a series of ripples that spreads far across the once peaceful body of water. *Gideon* was just such a case.

The series of ripples caused by *Gideon* began first with the effect that the decision had upon Gideon himself and the Bay County criminal justice system. Beyond this personal and most narrow of consequences, the next ring of waves represented the impact of the case on the state of Florida. Not only was Florida forced to provide adequate assistance of counsel for all defendants accused of committing a felony, but the state was also forced to deal with the several thousand inmates in the state's prison system who, like Gideon, were convicted without counsel.

Gideon v. Wainwright is a truly historic Supreme Court decision because the ripples that it produced moved far beyond the first splash in the water. The case started a series of decisions that related to the Sixth Amendment's right to counsel guarantee. *Gideon* also raised many critical questions about how far its narrow holding would reach. The *Gideon* decision raised many different kinds of issues that needed clarification and possible expansion. Should the guarantee of right to counsel be extended to other, less serious, categories of offenses? How early within the criminal process should the defendant be afforded a right to legal counsel? At which stages in the proceedings must a lawyer be made available to the indigent defendant—at the lineup, initial appearance, or grand jury, for example? Since the defendant must be represented by a competent attorney, how shall this level of performance be legally defined? How may a defendant constitutionally waive his right to counsel if he wishes to defend himself?

In the years since *Gideon*, the Supreme Court has attempted to answer all these complex questions relating to the Sixth Amendment's right to counsel protection. This collection of issues has generated thousands of appeals to the Supreme Court, many of which were granted certiorari, and has resulted in a significant body of right to coun-

The Burger Court of the late 1970s: (clockwise from upper left) William H. Rehnquist, Harry A. Blackmun, Lewis F. Powell, Jr., John Paul Stevens, Thurgood Marshall, Potter Stewart, Warren E. Burger, William J. Brennan, Jr., and Byron R. White

sel protection decisions. The Court has not always followed a straight path in dealing with these questions. In fact, the late Warren E. Burger and early William H. Rehnquist Courts in the 1980s and early 1990s provided several decisions that reversed earlier gains in several of these areas.

EXTENSION TO LESSER CRIMES

One of the first issues that arose after the *Gideon* decision was whether to extend the ruling to *all* criminal cases where the defendant faces the possibility of imprisonment. From *Powell v. Alabama* to the more recent *Argersinger v. Hamlin*, the Court moved from extending a right to counsel to only those defendants facing the death penalty to extending it to broader and less serious categories of defendants. The *Gideon* case widened the scope of application of Sixth Amendment guarantees from capital offenses (e.g., *Powell v. Alabama*) to all types of felonies. A felony is generally defined as a serious offense in which the defendant faces imprisonment for at least a year in a state prison. The crime Gideon was accused of was attempting to break into a pool hall, a felony under Florida law; Gideon's sentence was five years in the state penitentiary.

After Gideon's Supreme Court victory, people immediately asked whether defendants who were convicted of lesser crimes, such as misdemeanors and petty offenses, and faced imprisonment in local and county jails for lesser amounts of time than Gideon had—usually from thirty days to one year—were also guaranteed right to counsel. Could these defendants who were denied legal assistance not also have profited from the assistance of counsel? Were Justice Black's reasons for supporting *Gideon* not equally applicable to less serious criminal matters where the accused faced a loss of freedom, albeit a much smaller one?

Nine years after the *Gideon* decision, the Supreme Court decision *Argersinger v. Hamlin* in 1972 answered these questions. In a majority opinion by Justice William O. Douglas, the Court answered yes to these questions and expanded the scope of the Sixth Amendment's guarantees of effective assistance of counsel to any case where the defendant faced the possibility of imprisonment. In his opinion, Justice Douglas noted that the *Powell* and *Gideon* precedents involved felonies. "But their rationale has relevance to any criminal trial, where an accused is deprived of liberty. *Powell* and *Gideon* suggest that there are certain fundamental rights applicable to all such criminal prosecutions. . . . The requirement of counsel may well be necessary for a fair trial even in a petty offense prosecution."[1]

In essence, the rule that emerged from Douglas's opinion was more concerned with not limiting a precedent than with expanding the right to counsel issue. Justices Powell and Rehnquist differed with Douglas, arguing that right to counsel should be viewed primarily as a due process issue requiring fundamental fairness. In other words, legal counsel is needed in order to assure a fair trial in any criminal matter, regardless of the seriousness of the charge. Some legal scholars have characterized the *Argersinger* opinion as advocating "A *Betts*-type rule in which a judge would decide whether, based on the nature of the offense, the characteristics of the defendant, and the likelihood of a prison sentence, counsel should be appointed in a specific petty case."[2]

The Supreme Court was well aware of the staggering implications of expanding the coverage of the right to counsel provision to less serious cases. After *Gideon*, state and local justice systems had begun the complicated and expensive task of ensuring that all indigents were offered the assistance of effective counsel. Since most estimates showed nearly 80 percent of these defendants were unable to afford counsel and thus required state assistance, the problem was of staggering proportions.

By 1972, when *Argersinger* was decided, the local justice systems had just begun to operate effective public defender and assigned counsel programs for indigent defendants. When *Argersinger* added people accused of misdemeanors to the list, the local justice systems faced a four- to sixfold increase in the number of potential cases requiring public legal assistance.[3]

While there had long been clear documentation that recognized the critical role of counsel in these less serious cases, the local officials shuddered at the thought of providing counsel to the hundreds of thousands of defendants now entitled to representation by competent attorneys. By encouraging indigents accused of misdemeanors to waive their right to counsel and by streamlining public defender and assigned counsel programs, local justice systems have spent the years after *Argersinger* trying to satisfy its mandate.

In 1979, the Supreme Court, led by Chief Justice Burger and Associate Justice Rehnquist, was able to put the brakes on right to counsel extensions and even force a slight retrenchment, or curtailment, of the ruling. Again, the Court's reaction to the widening scope of *Gideon* has not always moved forward in a single direction. On occasion, especially in the more conservative Court of the late 1970s and early 1980s, retrenchments were evident.

In *Scott v. Illinois*, for example, the Supreme Court put limits on the *Argersinger* decision. In this 1979 ruling, the Court held that a right to counsel did not apply in trials of lesser offenses where no sentence of imprisonment was imposed, even though such a sentence could have been. Justice Rehnquist wrote the *Scott v. Illinois* opinion for a sharply divided court; the vote was five to four. In that opinion, Rehnquist stated that *Argersinger* did not require reversal of a defendant's conviction for shoplifting, a crime for which he was fined fifty dollars, even though he had not been provided an attorney and had faced a possible sentence of up to a year in jail.[4]

EXTENSION TO EARLIER STAGES IN THE PROCEEDINGS

One issue that the Warren Court failed to identify and comment upon in its *Gideon* decision was exactly when the right to counsel would be made available to a defendant. The question of at what critical stage of the proceedings an indigent defendant would be granted his attorney to begin his defense was left unanswered. It was in the famous *Escobedo* and *Miranda* decisions, handed down a few years after *Gideon*, that the "critical stage" issue began to be clarified.

The *Escobedo v. Illinois* case, decided in 1964, linked the Fifth Amendment's privilege against self-incrimination with the right to counsel guarantees of the Sixth Amendment. The decision held that a suspect had absolute right to the assistance of counsel following his arrest and during the subsequent police interrogation. The Court reasoned that a defendant unprotected by the advice of counsel may offer incriminating statements to the police during questioning. Therefore, whenever a defendant requests an attorney—even at the earliest time of detention—prior to any court appearance, the police must honor that request, cease

Two years after Escobedo v. Illinois*, which extended the right to counsel to immediately after arrest, Danny Escobedo listens to his court-appointed lawyer in an unrelated case.*

their interrogation, and provide the defendant an attorney.

Two years later, the historic case of *Miranda v. Arizona* extended the protection offered by a defendant's counsel even further. The Warren Court declared that the presence of counsel was necessary. They stated, "we hold that an individual held for interrogation must be clearly informed that he has the right to consult with a lawyer and to have the lawyer with him during interrogation."[5]

The *Miranda* case moved beyond *Escobedo* because it required the police to take the initiative to notify a defendant of his rights after his arrest. Those rights included a Fifth Amendment right to remain silent and a Sixth Amendment right to an attorney provided by the state. The public has often viewed *Miranda* as a decision that hampered police in their efforts to obtain confessions. However, it is constitutionally crucial to require the state to inform the defendant that he may say nothing for the record until he has an attorney to represent him.

Although the 1966 *Miranda* decision clearly established a defendant's right to be notified of his right to counsel as soon as he is taken into custody, the Supreme Court still had to clarify at which "critical stages" of the proceedings an attorney had to be available to assist a defendant.

Before a defendant makes his initial appearance before a judge, he has the right to have his attorney present during any interrogation. In 1967, the Supreme Court added the police lineup as another critical stage requiring legal assistance. The cases of *U.S. v. Wade* and its state counterpart, *Gilbert v. California*, held that any in-court identification of defendants based on a pretrial lineup conducted without the presence of the defendant's attorney was inadmissible as evidence. As with so many other Warren Court decisions affecting the rights of persons accused of crimes, the *Gilbert* and *Wade* holdings were also undercut by subsequent Burger and Rehnquist Court decisions.

By the early 1970s the Burger Court made it clear that the *Gideon*-inspired right to counsel would not take effect until "formal prosecutorial proceedings were under way." Justice Potter Stewart clarified this point in the *Kirby v. Illinois* decision when he emphasized that the critical stages began only after the prosecutorial forces had gathered evidence and indicted a defendant. He wrote that "It is at this point therefore that marks the commencement of the criminal prosecutions to which alone the explicit guarantees of the Sixth Amendment are applicable."[6]

In his 1972 article, "The Right to Counsel," Professor William Beaney traced the right of counsel guarantee at all stages of a felony proceeding. He carefully illustrated the necessity for an attorney's presence at the initial appearance, grand jury, preliminary hearing, arraignment, trial, and, to a limited degree, at the appeals stage. Despite the legal victories for the extension of right to counsel at all critical stages of the criminal process, the actual quality of legal defense offered indigent defendants has not kept pace. Professor Beaney described this disappointing phenomenon: "Too often counsel is appointed too late to adequately protect his client. Similarly appointed counsel is frequently overburdened and under-paid. Seldom does he have adequate investigatory resources to prepare his case."[7]

It is important to note, in concluding the examination of the "critical stages" issue, that despite the holdings of the three companion cases decided along with *Gideon* in March 1963, the Supreme Court a decade later also began to retrench in its extension of the right to counsel to the appellate process. In *Ross v. Moffit*, decided in 1974, the

Court held that the state's constitutional obligation to provide appointed counsel for indigents appealing their convictions did not extend past the point where their right to appeal had been effectively exhausted.[8]

DEFINING EFFECTIVE ASSISTANCE OF COUNSEL

In the years that have followed the *Gideon* decision, the Supreme Court has ruled on a defendant's right to an attorney at all critical stages of a criminal proceeding and on the right to legal assistance for nearly all categories of crimes. What about defining and establishing a constitutionally acceptable level of performance for a defendant's lawyer? In other words, what exactly does the Supreme Court mean when they guarantee criminal defendants the right to "effective assistance of counsel"? What level of legal performance or competence will be found by the courts to be above or below an acceptable standard? Because the U.S. justice system relies on the presence of two competent legal adversaries, each arguing opposite sides of a case before a neutral judge, *both* sides must perform at some standard of effectiveness.

Establishing a clear, workable standard of professional competence for defense attorneys has been a most elusive and challenging assignment. One factor complicating this difficult task is the Supreme Court's after-the-fact analysis of a lawyer's performance. Appellate court judges appear to use a different standard of performance from trial court judges, who frequently see incompetent defense attorneys losing their clients' cases before their very eyes. When appellate court judges review a lawyer's performance by reading the trial transcript, it is difficult to detect the subtle failings and many acts of omission. It is therefore rare for an appellate judge, absent at the initial trial, to appreciate a lawyer's incomplete trial preparation and shortsighted investigation—mistakes that ultimately undermine a defendant's chance for acquittal.

This confusing state of affairs has led the courts to create a set of professional standards so vague as to be nearly impossible to apply on a consistent basis. Like many other professional groups, the legal profession has had difficulty enforcing standards and holding accountable members of the profession who fall below these limits. The American Bar Association itself has investigated repeated complaints of its failure to discipline its membership.

In addition to establishing and enforcing workable standards of competence specifically for criminal defense lawyers, there are the practical difficulties of implementing the *Gideon* mandate. With at least three-fourths of all defendants dependent on the state for competent counsel, local governments have felt the weight of an awesome financial burden. Public defender and appointed counsel programs have experienced crippling cutbacks. The results include staggering caseloads for each attorney and less money for private attorneys assigned to state cases. Whether these working conditions have caused them to perform below the required standards, in behavior that has been described as making a "mockery of justice," is a question that only the appellate courts, and ultimately the Supreme Court, can answer.

What then has the Supreme Court said about

what is meant by "effective assistance of counsel" as required by the Sixth Amendment? The question was first addressed even before *Gideon*, in *Powell v. Alabama*. The judge in the original trial in Scottsboro first appointed the entire local bar to help the young defendants. When no one stepped forward, the judge then selected an inexperienced Tennessee attorney a few days before the trial commenced. In reviewing these two halfhearted attempts to supply the defendants with the barest form of legal defense, the Supreme Court pointed out that when a court is required to appoint counsel for a capital offense, that duty "is not discharged by an assignment at such a time or under such circumstances as to preclude the giving of *effective* aid in the preparation and trial of the case."[9]

When Chief Justice Earl Warren stepped down from the Supreme Court in 1970, the competence of counsel issue became more difficult to challenge. Several decisions during the 1970s rejected efforts by defendants who wished to challenge their convictions because of supposedly incompetent legal defense. In *Tollet v. Henderson*, decided in 1973, the Court held that defendants had to assume a certain degree of risk that their attorneys would make some ordinary or minor errors in attempting to obtain their freedom. If these errors did not combine to create a "mockery of justice," then they would not be sufficient basis for reversing a conviction.[10]

This trend toward taking a more critical view of defendants' claims of having received less than competent counsel was continued by the Supreme Court during the 1970s and the 1980s, reaching its high-water mark with two cases decided in 1984.

Justice Sandra Day O'Connor, whose majority opinion in Strickland v. Washington *continued a less defendant-friendly trend in the Supreme Court*

In the first case—*Strickland v. Washington*—the Court, in an opinion written by Justice Sandra Day O'Connor, held that even if a lawyer's errors were so serious that counsel was not functioning as guaranteed by the Sixth Amendment, a conviction should not be reversed unless the defendant shows "there is a reasonable probability that but for counsel's unprofessional errors, the result of the proceeding would have been different."[11] The Supreme Court established a two-prong test that had to be met before a conviction could be overturned based upon the ineffective assistance of counsel argument: (1) the defendant must show deficient performance by the trial attorney; and (2) the defendant must show that the deficient performance resulted in sufficient prejudice to him.

The *Strickland* decision sent a clear message to the lower courts that in any appeal of a conviction based on a challenge to the defense attorney's performance, the Supreme Court maintained a strong presumption that the lawyer's conduct was constitutionally adequate. The Supreme Court explained its position by asserting that "It is all too tempting for a defendant to second-guess counsel's assistance after conviction or adverse sentence, and it is all too easy for a court, examining counsel's defense after it has proved unsuccessful, to conclude that a particular act or omission of counsel was unreasonable."[12]

The other case decided in 1984, on the same day as *Strickland*, was *U.S. v. Cronic*. In this case, the Supreme Court unanimously decided that an appeals court was wrong to conclude that a defendant had been denied the right to counsel because the appointed counsel lacked criminal law experience and did not have much time to prepare for trial. Justice Stevens emphasized that these inadequacies must be supported by evidence of serious errors by the lawyer to the degree that they were so prejudicial as to deny the defendant a fair trial.[13]

Today, it seems that the Supreme Court is still willing to follow the broad guidelines of the *Gideon* decision. However, when it comes to the standards used to determine if a defendant has been denied "effective assistance of counsel," the Court continues to follow the *Strickland* and *Cronic* decisions. That is, the Court will be convinced in only the most grievous of circumstances that a defense lawyer's incompetent performance created such a prejudicial situation that the defendant was denied a fair trial.

WAIVING THE RIGHT TO COUNSEL

Since *Gideon*, the Supreme Court has also had to decide what to do when a defendant refuses to accept the assistance of counsel and waives his Sixth Amendment rights. The definitive case on this unusual yet important issue is *Faretta v. California*, decided in 1975. In this case, Justice Potter Stewart, writing the majority opinion, explained that defendants do have the right to conduct their own defense and the right to reject counsel appointed to represent them. Stewart wrote that "it is one thing to hold that every defendant, rich or poor, has the right to the assistance of counsel, and quite another to say that a state may compel a defendant to accept a lawyer he does not want."[14]

Even more important than granting the right to refuse counsel is the establishment of procedures to ensure that the defendant has made an unco-

In 1975, Justice Potter Stewart wrote the majority opinion for a case that supported the right of a defendent to refuse counsel.

erced, rational decision to reject legal assistance. The *Faretta* case and several other federal decisions have combined to require the court to follow carefully this procedure before a waiver can be accepted:

> 1. Advise the defendant that he has the right to retain counsel and that time will be allowed for him to do so if need be, and if he is indigent, counsel will be appointed for him at no cost.
> 2. Ascertain that the defendant knowingly, intelligently, and unambiguously waives his right.
> 3. Make a record that each of the above precautions has been taken.[15]

Since so many defendants plead guilty without the assistance of counsel, it is especially important that trial court judges ensure that the waiver is being made intelligently and in compliance with these noted procedures. It is very rare for a defendant to waive his right to counsel and then choose to defend himself in a jury trial. The waiver is most typically done by defendants who, shortly after their arrest, believe that it is in their best interests to accept the prosecution's offer of a lighter sentence in return for a plea of guilty. The general rule understood by most defendants and prosecutors is that the earlier the plea arrangement is finalized, the more advantageous the settlement for the defendant; simply stated, the sooner the plea, the lesser the sentence. Although trial court judges may realize that these waivers of counsel, done in conjunction with a plea bargain, may be beneficial to the defendant, they nevertheless must move cautiously to make sure that the defendant understood what he was doing and that no coercion was involved.

IMPACT ON COSTS AND QUALITY OF DEFENSE

Post-*Gideon* decisions have clarified such questions as what levels of crimes are to be covered by the *Gideon* ruling, when and during which proceedings the right to counsel applies, and how competent this legal assistance must be. Beyond these important constitutional issues is the equally important question of what the practical consequences of the *Gideon* decision have been.

Since 1963, when Clarence Gideon was granted his retrial and all felony defendants were given the right to counsel, hundreds of thousands of indigent defendants have been able to obtain free legal assistance at public expense. The *Gideon* decision has had an enormous financial impact on state and local government. Unfortunately, many jurisdictions have not been able to fulfill their constitutional obligations to provide the Sixth Amendment guarantees. In 1973, David Bazelon, former chief judge of the District of Columbia Circuit Court of Appeals, wrote that "the battle for justice is being lost in the trenches of the criminal courts where the promise of *Gideon* and *Argersinger* goes unfulfilled. The casualties of those defeats are easy to identify. . . . The prime casualties are defendants accused of street crimes, virtually all of whom are poor, uneducated, and unemployed."[16]

The same depressing picture of legal services for the poor was found in another 1973 study. The National Legal Aid and Defender Association conducted a sixteen-month nationwide study assessing the delivery of defense services to indigents in three thousand counties across the nation. Their report concluded that "The scope of representation provided for indigent defendants in many jurisdictions does not meet specific constitutional directives of the Supreme Court."[17]

One of the clearest indicators of the crisis in defense services caused by the requirements of the *Gideon* decision are the fiscal problems noted by Professor Norman Lefstein in his report to the ABA Committee on Legal Aid and Indigent Defendants:

> In Massachusetts over $3 million is owed to the private bar for work performed during the past three years.
>
> In February the Missouri Public Defender Commission announced that it had spent its entire appointed counsel budget for the fiscal year ending June 30th and could no longer pay attorney fees and expenses.
>
> In West Virginia private lawyers are owed fees totaling $170,000 for work performed in 1978-79.
>
> In one Louisiana county, the private bar fees of more than $240,000 have not been paid and there is no apparent carryover to the next year.
>
> In Greenville, S.C., the county commissioners voted to discontinue the $240,000 spent by the county for a mixed-defender system and replace it with a $90,000 contract for five part-time lawyers. Similar proposals are presently pending in Oregon, Oklahoma, and Pennsylvania.
>
> Cases in Florida, California, Georgia, Massachusetts, Montana, Oklahoma, Missouri, Oregon, Nebraska, Iowa, Alabama, and Tennessee are raising questions of

> adequate compensation, improper reduction of fees, involuntary servitude, and the denial of due process for their clients.[18]

Given the reality of these financial obstacles to equal justice, one must wonder what impact they have had upon the very basis of our system of justice. As law professor Richard Klein points out, "If either side is so disadvantaged, underfunded, or overburdened that it cannot function in this expected manner, then the adversarial process has failed."[19] When one compares the ability of the prosecutor to spend monies on such items as laboratory analyses by police chemists, various expert witnesses, and special investigators conducting laborious inquiries with the equivalent investigative services available to indigent defendants who must rely upon public legal assistance, one cannot help but wonder about the realities of this justice system for indigent defendants.

Recent decisions in Iowa and Illinois, however, have shown that the spirit behind the *Gideon* decision is still alive. An Iowa appellate court, in the case of *Hulse v. Wifirat*, held that a court-appointed attorney is entitled to full compensation for his reasonably necessary services as gauged by ordinary and customary charges for like services in the community, and that no discount is required based on attorney's duty to represent the poor. Similarly, an Illinois court ruled that the standard of "reasonableness" used for the assessment of fees for appointed counsel was abused by the court when it awarded fees of less than eight dollars per hour.[20]

All three branches of government—judicial, executive, and legislative—at both the state and national level, will be faced with renewing their commitment to honor the promises made in *Gideon* guaranteeing that all defendants, regardless of economic condition, will receive the full protection of the Sixth Amendment's right to effective assistance of counsel.

Chapter 7

RECENT CHALLENGES

The United States employs the so-called adversary system of justice, combined with the requirements of due process. Thus, before a defendant can lose his freedom, a prosecutor must convince an unbiased judge or jury that the defendant is guilty beyond a reasonable doubt. It is believed that through this struggle between these two legal adversaries—prosecutor and defense attorney—the justice system will operate most fairly. For this legal system to work fairly, it is clear that having a lawyer is essential. As Judge Schaefer of the Illinois Supreme Court once said, "Of all the rights that an accused person has, the right to be represented by counsel is by far the most pervasive, for it affects his ability to assert any other rights he may have."[1]

Given an adversary system and the critical importance of assistance of competent counsel, it is no surprise that the *Gideon v. Wainwright* decision has proved to be an historic Supreme Court case. This decision entitled the original defendant, Clarence Gideon, to a retrial, with the assistance of counsel. It also entitled all defendants, regardless of their economic condition, accused of felony crimes in state courts across the nation, to right to counsel provisions of the Sixth Amendment.

The implications of *Gideon* created a constitutional obligation on the states to furnish legal defense for indigent defendants through either public defenders or assigned counsel. The quality of this defense must be at a level of competence that ensures that justice is done.

In addition to being an adversary system, the U.S. legal system is also a common-law system. It depends heavily on legal precedent, but it has the capacity to overturn a precedent if the precedent is found to be no longer acceptable. In the *Gideon* decision, the Supreme Court directly overruled an earlier case, *Betts v. Brady*, decided only twenty years earlier. The *Gideon* decision remains a strong precedent guaranteeing right to counsel in state criminal cases, yet its growth as a legal precedent has not been without setbacks.

The following is a quick overview of the somewhat erratic pattern of defendants' rights cases since *Gideon*. The *Argersinger*[2] decision in 1972 extended *Gideon*'s right to counsel protection to any case where the defendant could possibly receive a prison or jail sentence. This was limited seven years later in *Scott v. Illinois*,[3] which held that the right to counsel did not apply to trials of lesser offenses where no sentence was imposed even though one could have been. Another example of the undermining of *Gideon* related to guaranteeing counsel at critical pretrial stages of the proceedings. In 1967 in the *Wade*[4] and *Gilbert*[5] deci-

After winning his appeal to the Supreme Court and his case on retrial, Clarence Gideon speaks on the radio with talk-show host Larry King.

sions, it appeared that the right to counsel was to be extended to all police lineups, but in 1972 the Burger Court eroded the impact of these decisions. In *Kirby v. Illinois*[6] the Court held that the right to counsel did not apply to persons who had not yet been indicted but who had to appear in a lineup. A final example relates to the critical question of what the Court defines as "competent assistance of counsel." In 1984 the Supreme Court apparently compromised the promise of *Gideon*. In establishing an acceptable level of performance that was easily satisfied, the Court made it extremely difficult for a defendant to challenge the quality of his legal defense. In *Strickland v. Washington*[7] the Court held that a defendant received effective assistance of counsel despite the fact that his attorney gave up and failed to represent the defendant vigorously in a capital case. Also in 1984, the Court held in *U.S. v. Cronic*[8] that a real estate lawyer with no trial experience who had twenty-five days to prepare to try a complicated case, did not fall below the standards required for "effective assistance of counsel."

Despite the erosive effect of these decisions, *Gideon* still remains an important precedent guaranteeing the Sixth Amendment's right to counsel provisions in state criminal cases. One important aspect of *Gideon* is that the Supreme Court was willing to step into the state judicial systems across the nation and impose a federal standard of due process of law that challenged the existing level of legal protection offered defendants. Although by 1963 most states had already provided indigent defendants with a guaranteed right to counsel, there were nevertheless several states that failed to comply, and no clear-cut national standard. The *Gideon* decision, therefore, is an excellent example of the power of the federal judiciary to act when they believe the states have failed to provide the necessary due process guarantees needed to ensure that all of the nation's courts are providing fundamental fairness.

Where does the right to counsel protection guaranteed in the *Gideon* decision stand today? Recent cases such as *Strickland* and *Cronic* create doubts about its future efficacy. Much depends on the attitude and ideology of newer members of the Supreme Court. It is also very likely that there will be several retirements in the near future. It is unlikely that a radical change in the *Gideon* requirement of counsel holding will occur—especially not a direct reversal—but there have been numerous cases that have undermined the quality of required legal defense.

Because of the fiscal crises facing most state and local governments, their present and future capability to fund viable public defender and assigned counsel programs is of paramount concern. *Wolff v. Ruddy*,[9] which permits states to require lawyers to provide legal assistance to impoverished defendants without compensation or face serious repercussions such as possible disbarment, is one dark cloud on the horizon for officials concerned with the quality of indigent defense. It is frightening to imagine the quality of legal defense offered by a lawyer coerced into acting as counsel in a criminal case. How aggressive and comprehensive will that legal defense be? Can we expect an attorney, who is receiving little or no compensation, to spend long days and nights investigating the case, interviewing witnesses, and preparing for trial? Future indigent defendants assigned counsel by the state may not be able to expect very much beyond minimally acceptable levels of performance from their counselors.

Although these erosions and fiscal uncertainties may have taken some of the glitter off Clarence Earl Gideon's victory and clouded the future, *Gideon v. Wainwright* remains a major Supreme Court decision and a milestone in the historic development of the Bill of Rights generally and the right to counsel specifically. In the words of Justice Hugo L. Black, "the Supreme Court has given significant expression [in *Gideon*] to two of this country's deepest ideals and aspirations—a fair trial and just treatment of the poor and disadvantaged." The *Gideon v. Wainwright* decision shows the power of a single individual, with perseverance and courage, to change the course of legal history.

SOURCE NOTES

CHAPTER 1

1. Anthony Lewis, *Gideon's Trumpet* (New York: Random House, 1964), 102.
2. From transcript of record pp. 23–24, Gideon v. Wainwright, 372 US 335 (1963).
3. Lewis, 60.
4. David O'Brien, *Storm Center: The Supreme Court in American Politics*, 3rd ed. (New York: Norton and Company, 1993), 248.
5. Ibid., 172.
6. Lewis, 4.
7. Ibid., 39.
8. Bernard Schwartz, *Super Chief: Earl Warren and His Supreme Court—A Judicial Biography* (New York: NYU Press, 1983), 458–59.

CHAPTER 2

1. 316 US 455 (1942). [This citation means that this case can be found in volume 316 of the official Supreme Court reports and on page 455 of that

volume. The date in parentheses is the year the case was decided.]
2. Robert Herman et al., *Counsel for the Poor* (Lexington, Mass.: Lexington Books, 1977), 11.
3. 287 US 45 (1932).
4. Dan T. Carter, *Scottsboro: A Tragedy of the American South* (New York: Oxford University Press, 1971), 18.
5. 287 US 69 (1932).
6. Ibid., 71.
7. 304 US 458 (1932).
8. 316 US 472 (1942).
9. Ibid., 463.
10. Yale Kamisar, "Gideon v. Wainwright: A Quarter Century Later," 10 *Pace Law Review* 327 (Spring 1990): 350.
11. 351 US 12 (1956).
12. Francis Allen, "The Supreme Court, Federalism, and State Systems of Criminal Justice," 8 *DePaul Law Review* 213 (1959): 230–31.
13. 363 US 697, 704 (1960).

CHAPTER 3

1. Robert Shogan. *A Question of Judgment* (Indianapolis: Bobbs-Merrill, 1972), 74.
2. Laura Kalman, *Abe Fortas* (New Haven: Yale University Press, 1990), 184.
3. Ibid.
4. Ibid., 182.
5. Anthony Lewis, *Gideon's Trumpet* (New York: Random House, 1964), 81.
6. Brief for Petitioner Clarence Earl Gideon v. H. G. Cochran, Jr. U.S. Supreme Court, October term 1962, No. 155 p. 8.
7. Ibid.
8. Lewis, 167–68.
9. Lewis, 149.

10. "Gideon v. Wainwright Revisited—What Does the Right to Counsel Guarantee Today," 10 *Pace Law Review* 327 at 347.

CHAPTER 4

1. Anthony Lewis, *Gideon's Trumpet* (New York: Random House, 1964), 182.
2. Ibid., 193.
3. 372 US 353 (1963).
4. 304 US 458 (1938).
5. 372 US 335 at 339 (1963).
6. Ibid. at 348.
7. Ibid.
8. Ibid.
9. Ibid. at 350.
10. Philip Kurland, *The Supreme Court Review—1963 Edition* (Chicago: University of Chicago Press, 1964).
11. Abe Krash, "The Right to a Lawyer: The Implications of Gideon v. Wainwright," 39 *Notre Dame Lawyer* 150 (February 1964): 153.
12. Ibid.

CHAPTER 5

1. 372 US 487 (1963).
2. 372 US 477 (1963).
3. 372 US 353 (1963).
4. Richard Klein. "The Emperor Gideon Has No Clothes," 13 *Hastings Constitutional Law Quarterly* 625 (Summer 1986): 721.
5. 351 US 12 (1956).
6. "The Supreme Court, 1962 Term," 77 *Harvard Law Review* 103: 107.
7. Klein, 723.
8. Anthony Lewis, *Gideon's Trumpet* (New York: Random House, 1964), 239.
9. Ibid., 250.

10. Abe Krash, "The Right to a Lawyer: The Implications of Gideon v. Wainwright," 39 *Notre Dame Lawyer* 150 (February 1964): 154.
11. Lewis, 215.
12. Lee Silverstein, "The Continuing Impact of Gideon v. Wainwright," 51 *American Bar Association Journal* 1023 (November 1965): 1024.
13. Lewis, 217.
14. Silverstein, 1023.

CHAPTER 6

1. Elder Witt, *The Supreme Court and Individual Rights* (Washington, D.C.: Congressional Quarterly, 1988), 206.
2. William Beaney, "The Right to Counsel," in *The Rights of the Accused*, ed. Stuart Nagel (Beverly Hills, Calif.: Sage Publications, 1972), 150.
3. Paul Wice, *Chaos in the Courthouse* (New York: Praeger Publishers, 1985). Sourcebook of Criminal Statistics 1975–85. Washington, D.C. U.S. Department of Justice, National Criminal Justice Information and Statistics Service, 1986.
4. 440 US 367 (1979).
5. 384 US 436 at 466 (1966).
6. 406 US 682 at 689 (1972).
7. Beaney, 169.
8. 417 US 600 (1974).
9. Powell v. Alabama, 287 US 45 at 71 (1932).
10. 411 US 258 (1973).
11. 466 US 668 at 694 (1984).
12. Ibid., 689.
13. 466 US 648 (1984).
14. 422 US 806 at 832 (1975).
15. Beaney, 164.
16. David Bazelon, "Defective Assistance of Counsel," 23 *University of Cincinnati* 1 (1973): 811.
17. Richard Klein, "The Emperor Gideon Has No

Clothes: The Empty Promise of the Constitutional Right to Effective Assistance of Counsel," 13 *Hastings Constitutional Law Quarterly* 625 (Summer 1986): 657.
18. Norman Lefstein, "Criminal Defense Services for the Poor: Methods and Programs for Providing Legal Representation and the Need for Adequate Financing," Report to the American Bar Association Committee on Legal Aid and Indigent Defendants. (August 1981), p. G-2.
19. Ibid.
20. Wice, 86.

CHAPTER 7

1. Walter Schaefer, "Federalism and State Criminal Procedure," 70 *Harvard Law Review* 1 (1956): 8.
2. Argersinger v. Hamlin, 407 US 25 (1972).
3. 440 US 367 (1979).
4. U.S. v. Wade, 388 US 218 (1967).
5. Gilbert v. California, 388 US 263 (1967).
6. 406 US 682 (1972).
7. 466 US 688 (1984).
8. 466 US 648 (1984).
9. 617 SW 2nd 64 (1981) Missouri.

FOR FURTHER READING

The most famous and highly praised account of the *Gideon v. Wainwright* decision is the Pulitzer Prize–winning book by Anthony Lewis, *Gideon's Trumpet* (New York: Random House, 1964). (It was also published later, in 1989, by Vintage.) Not only does Lewis's book chronicle Clarence Earl Gideon's historic legal struggle, but it also provides an excellent overview of how the Supreme Court operates. Another book that provides a clear and even more comprehensive picture of the Supreme Court and the federal court system is David O'Brien's *Storm Center: The Supreme Court in American Politics* (New York: Norton and Company, 1990).

An excellent book on the *Powell v. Alabama* decision, *Gideon*'s important precedent, is *Scottsboro Boys* (New York: Oxford University Press, 1971), by Dan Carter, a University of Maryland historian. The *Gideon* case is also eloquently discussed as part of the Warren Court's "Due Process

Revolution" in Fred Graham's *The Self-Inflicted Wound* (New York: Hayden Book Company, 1970); this work has also been reissued under a new title, *The Due Process Revolution.* A more legalistic and sophisticated treatise is Craig Bradley's *The Failure of the Criminal Procedure Revolution* (Philadelphia: University of Pennsylvania Press, 1993).

Those wishing to learn more about Gideon's famous lawyer, Abe Fortas, are urged to read Laura Kalman's *Abe Fortas: A Biography* (New Haven, Conn.: Yale University Press, 1990). For further reading on the justice who authored the majority opinion in *Gideon*, there is Roger Newman's recent biography, *Hugo Black* (New York: Pantheon Books, 1994). Finally, Richard Harris's *Freedom Spent* (Boston: Little, Brown, 1976) illustrates how difficult it can be to fully exercise one's constitutional rights.

Page numbers in *italics* indicate illustrations.

sscca 345
.73056
W633